DATE DUE

NOV 17 '98			
JAN 07 '00			
MAR 1 3 2002			

GUADALCANAL DIARY

•

The desperate battle for Guadalcanal and the Solomon Islands was a crucial turning point of World War II.

Among the eyewitnesses to this daring campaign in the Pacific was war correspondent Richard Tregaskis. Tregaskis was with the U.S. Marines when they landed on the Japanese-held island of Guadalcanal in the summer of 1942. He spent seven dangerous weeks with the front-line troops, eating, sleeping, sweating—and avoiding enemy snipers in the trees. He also kept a diary, in which he described the island's takeover by American forces against overwhelming odds.

His diary was the basis for this book—a vivid, moving, often humorous chronicle. It brings to life one of the most vital military campaigns in American history.

GUADALCANAL DIARY

•

BY
RICHARD TREGASKIS

RANDOM HOUSE NEW YORK

Published as Landmark #55
by Random House in 1955.

First published in paperback as Landmark #14
by Random House in 1984.

Library of Congress Cataloging in Publication Data:
Tregaskis, Richard, 1916-1973.
  Guadalcanal diary.
  Includes index.
  1. World War, 1939-1945—Campaigns—Solomon Islands—Guadalcanal
Island. 2. Tregaskis, Richard, 1916-1973. 3. World War, 1939-1945—Personal
narratives, American. 4. United States. Marine Corps—History—World War,
1939-1945. 5. Guadalcanal Island (Solomon Islands)—History. I. Title.
D767.98.T7   1984   940.54'26 83-17662 ISBN: 0-394-86268-6

Photograph credits: United Press International, 12, 55 top, 64, 89, 112 top,
134, 143, 151; U.S. Army, 6; U.S. Department of Defense (Marine Corps), 36
top, 43, 55 bottom, 59, 90, 101 top, 112 bottom, 117, 122, 138, 160; U.S.
Marine Corps, 65; U.S. Navy, 5; Wide World Photos, ii, 36 bottom, 70, 75,
101 bottom, 147.

Manufactured in the United States of America

2 3 4 5 6 7 8 9 0

CONTENTS

•

GUADALCANAL DIARY

PREFACE

•

This edition of *Guadalcanal Diary* was prepared especially for the famous Landmark series for boys and girls. It was taken from the longer, original edition written while I was a war correspondent for International News Service in the Pacific. Since the Guadalcanal battle was still raging while I was writing that edition, I didn't know then whether we were going to win or lose. And since World War II was in its early stages, I didn't realize at the time how important the Guadalcanal campaign was to this country and the world. For the Landmark edition, I've written extra chapters to tell how the Battle of Guadalcanal fit into the history of the war in the Pacific—for Guadalcanal is now recognized as one of the most vital campaigns in all our history, worthy of rank with Valley Forge and Gettysburg.

—Richard Tregaskis

·1·
THE
PRELUDE TO
GUADALCANAL

On December 7, 1941, a day that will always be remembered by Americans, planes bearing the red sun insignia of Japan made a sneak attack on Pearl Harbor—and threw the United States into World War II. The biggest fight in our history started the next day as our Congress declared war on Japan and, three days after that, voted a state of war with Germany and Italy, Japan's allies in Europe.

The Japanese attack on Pearl Harbor, our main Pacific naval base, was delivered by bombers and torpedo planes roaring from aircraft carriers. The planes left mountains of flame and smoke behind them, crippled our Pacific fleet, sank five of our biggest warships,

The U.S.S. Arizona *burning after the Japanese attack on Pearl Harbor, December 7, 1941.*

and killed more than 3,000 American soldiers and sailors.

With a two-ocean war on our hands, and only small forces on land, sea, and air, we tackled a fight that seemed impossible to many people. We had only a million and a half men under arms. The Axis—Germany, Italy, and Japan—had ten times as many.

In the Pacific fast-moving Japanese troops

Victorious Japanese troops on Bataan.

swept to a stunning victory on Bataan, conquering a garrison of 20,000 American and Philippine soldiers. General Douglas MacArthur, the American commander, escaped to Australia, to take command there of new fighting forces as they came from the United States.

The Japanese armies, landing from ships and by parachute, attacked along a wide arc in the Pacific area. At the northern end of this arc, they battered a United States Marine garrison on Wake Island into submission. Farther south and west, they made short work of the British troops at Hong Kong and on the Malay Peninsula. They set British troops on the run in Burma and grabbed most of that country. They conquered the sprawling Dutch East Indies, rich in oil and rubber, and captured 98,000 prisoners. They invaded the Australian-controlled islands of New Guinea and the Solomons, dangerously close to Australia itself. It seemed there was no stopping the swarming millions of hard, well-trained Japanese and their powerful fleet with its well-coordinated fighters, bombers, and torpedo planes.

But on the other side of the world, beyond the Atlantic, an even more massive attack was roaring against Russia, which was then an ally of ours. Japan's ally, Germany, throwing in five million men with endless waves of tanks, artillery, and airplanes, had conquered most of Europe and part of Russia, almost to Moscow. The German bombers were wrecking the principal cities of England. In the North African desert, English and German tanks were locked in a massive struggle. President Franklin D. Roosevelt concluded that the toughest enemy was in Europe and Africa. As Commander-in-Chief of our forces, he decided that as our military strength grew, most of it should be sent across the Atlantic.

So the powerful Japanese foe had to be fought with one hand, and the weaker hand at that. More exactly, we had to fight the Japanese with one finger—because President Roosevelt's plan was to send nine-tenths of our fighting strength in men and materiel to the European-African area.

This meant we had precious little to fight with in the Pacific, especially in those early days when our factories were just beginning to produce planes, tanks, and guns in mass, and our plan to train fifteen million fighting men had just got under way. We had to battle for time. We had to meet the Japanese cautiously with small forces.

Fortunately the big Japanese air attack on Pearl Harbor hadn't sunk or even damaged any of our aircraft carriers, the big flattops that were destined to be our most important fighting vessels. We had four flattops in the Pacific: the *Saratoga*, the *Lexington*, the *Hornet*, and the *Enterprise*.

We also had a couple of naval task forces of moderate strength in the Pacific—a total of about 50 fighting ships, mostly cruisers and destroyers.

And we had two divisions of marines— about 40,000 men with artillery, tanks, and supply outfits. They were not completely trained, but they were marines and, being marines, they were ready to fight and eager to be the first to fight for us.

·2·
THE LANDING
PARTY

In March of 1942 the First Division of United States Marines was still in the United States. But they were getting ready to board ships to take them to the Pacific.

This plan, of course, was very secret. In the bustling headquarters of the Pacific Fleet in Pearl Harbor, only a handful of high officers knew that these troops were loading aboard ships. And none of those officers knew yet where the troops were going to be used. They knew only that somewhere along the 5,000-mile arc of the Japanese Pacific front, some of the troops would soon be landing under enemy guns. Wherever it happened, it had to be a surprise to the Japanese. Otherwise our small force would be overwhelmed and slaughtered.

Some of our naval officers guessed that this first American spearhead would be thrust into the Japanese flank somewhere north of Australia and New Zealand. Those two rich British dominions in the South Pacific were the anchor of British strength. If they fell, virtually all of the Pacific would be in the hands of the Japanese, making it very difficult for us to launch an offensive against Japan.

But exactly where our spearhead would strike was a question to be decided by the high command in Washington. The admirals and generals had long discussions as to where, north of Australia and New Zealand, the first American landing force should hit the Japanese. The high officers agreed that something had to be done quickly.

At Pearl Harbor we war correspondents at that time guessed too that there would be a landing party somewhere along the Japanese arc of conquest. We tried to get all the information we could so that we might be on hand if and when the landing party struck.

Meanwhile, we went out on the fighting ships of the United States Navy and watched and reported on naval battles with the Japanese. These furious fights of aircraft carrier fleets were bloody and damaging to both sides, but our carrier forces usually managed to win, and held back the Japanese tide of invasion sweeping across the Pacific.

Then, after the Battle of Midway in June of 1942, we correspondents were resting for a couple of days in Pearl Harbor when a friend of mine told me an exciting rumor: A landing party was going to hit soon.

I went straight to Commander Waldo Drake, one of Admiral Nimitz's staff, and asked for permission to go with the landing party. Drake said he knew of no landing party, but that he would check up. He went to Admiral Chester W. Nimitz, who was in command of the navy in the Pacific, and asked about it. Surprisingly enough, Admiral Nimitz gave me

Crew members of the damaged American aircraft carrier Yorktown *desperately try to save their ship during the Battle of Midway.*

secret orders to go on the landing party, then called by the code name "Watchtower."

Commander Drake cautioned me to say nothing about Watchtower. But I couldn't have told anyone where that landing party was heading. I simply didn't know, nor did Drake. Admiral Nimitz was probably the only man in Pearl Harbor who knew that the invasion was going to be made in the Solomon Islands, which are to the north of and between Australia and New Zealand. He was probably the only man on that base who knew the strange, unfamiliar names of the islands we would hit: Guadalcanal, Gavutu, Tanambogo.

With my orders in hand, I boarded the aircraft carrier *Enterprise,* outward bound for an unknown destination.

Our small task force steamed south and, after many days of sailing, arrived at a beautiful South Sea harbor called Nukualofa, in the Tonga Islands. When we sailed into the harbor, my heart seemed to leap up into my throat in excitement, for drawn up at anchor was a fleet of big transports loaded with marines!

That afternoon the *Enterprise* sailed out of Nukualofa, but without me. I had wangled a small boat to take me to a handsome troop transport, a converted ocean liner called the *Crescent City.* I had caught up with the landing party at last.

·3·
APPROACH

SUNDAY, JULY 26, 1942

This morning, it being Sunday, there were services on the port promenade. Benches had been arranged on the deck, facing a canvas backdrop on which a Red Cross flag was pinned. Father Francis W. Kelly of Philadelphia, a genial, smiling fellow with a faculty for plain talk, gave a sermon. It was his second for the day. He had just finished the "first shift," which was for Catholics. This one was for Protestants.

It was pleasant to stand and sing on the rolling deck with the blue panel of the moving sea on our left. There we could see two others of our fleet of transports rolling over the long swells, nosing into white surf.

The sermon dealt with duty and was obviously pointed toward our coming landing somewhere in Japanese-held territory. Father Kelly, who had been a preacher in a Pennsylvania mining town, pounded home the point.

After the services many of the men turned to the essential job of loading machine gun belts. Walking around the deck in the bright morning sun, I had to step around lads who were sitting on the former shuffleboard court, using a gadget that belted the cartridges automatically. All that had to be done was to feed them in. The boys seemed quite happy at the job.

In the luxurious modern after-lounge, preserved much as it had been when the ship was a passenger-freight liner, I found things quiet. One officer was reading a mystery novel as he sat on a modernistic couch done in red leather and chrome. A redheaded tank commander sat at one of the black-topped tables where until recently cocktails had been served to civilian passengers traveling between North and South America. He was writing an entry in his diary.

I spotted Major Cornelius P. Van Ess, the graying, earnest planning officer of this Second Regiment. He was unfolding a message that had just been given to him by a young naval lieutenant.

"Something to do with our destination?" I asked.

He smiled. "No," he said, "but I wish it were. I'd like to know too. Even the colonel doesn't yet know where we're headed."

After lunch I went back to the stateroom. I was passing the time of day with two of my roommates, a Red Cross worker named Albert Campbell and Father Kelly, when Dr. Garrison, the fourth occupant of the stateroom, rushed in puffing with excitement. A Los Angeles dentist in civilian life, Dr. John Garrison was a navy medical officer.

"A lot of ships just came up," he said, plunking his portly frame onto his bunk. "A whole navy. Better go look at 'em."

So we ambled out on deck and saw the horizon spotted with ships that were fanned out in a huge semicircle around us. There were transports and freight ships, cruisers, destroyers, and the long, high boxlike shapes of aircraft carriers.

Identification at that distance was difficult, but one thing is certain: We have made a rendezvous with the other and main part of our task forces. Totaling about seventy-five ships, it certainly is the largest and strongest assemblage of the Pacific war to date.

The thought that we are going into our adventure with weight and power behind us is cheering. And our adventure-to-come seems nearer than ever, for a new group of ships has merged with ours and we are now one huge force.

MONDAY, JULY 27, 1942

This morning there was much ado in the map-plastered office that Colonel John M. Arthur, the commanding officer, has set up at the edge of the after-lounge. A boat had come from one of the other ships, bringing dispatches. Word was whispered that it also brought the much-sought secret of our destination.

After lunch Dr. French Moore, a navy medical commander from San Francisco, told me that I was invited to come to the colonel's cabin before dinner for a spot of tea. I surmised that here I would get the news as to where we might be heading.

His regiment, the colonel explained, is not going to take part in the assault on Japanese-held territory. Only one battalion will be near the scene of action, and that will be a support force.

"So if you want to be in the forefront when the landing takes place," he said, "it might be wiser for you to shift to another ship."

I have come out here for action, so I agreed to make the shift. After dinner, in our blacked-out cabin, I packed my bags. It took some resolution to do the job, for this evening I learned that the forces I would join are going to attack the Japanese strongholds on Guadalcanal and Tulagi, in the Solomon Islands.

WEDNESDAY, JULY 29, 1942

I got the consent of Admiral Kelly Turner, commanding the landing operation, to move to another transport. The ship is one of the two that are to carry the assault troops landing on Guadalcanal. The Fifth Marine Regiment is to land first and seize the beachhead.

It was a shock to come close to my new ship. She is an ancient, angular horror with a black, dirty hull and patches of rust on her flanks. When I climbed the rope ladder up her high freeboard and set foot on deck, I could see that not all the Americans heading for the Solomons are traveling on the latest ships. I have certainly come from the best and newest to one of the oldest and most decrepit!

I went down one level and came to the cabin of Colonel LeRoy P. Hunt of Berkeley, California, commanding officer of the Fifth Marines' assault troops. Colonel Hunt's small room contained an iron bed, a couple of broken-down chairs, and a desk.

I talked to the colonel about the ship and his troops.

"Things are dirty here," he said. "There isn't enough water for cleaning up. My men are pretty unkempt, too, for the same reason. They look like gypsies. But," he added, "I think they'll fight. They've got it here." He tapped his chest in the region of the heart.

The colonel, a good-looking man of middle age, tall and well built, was quite serious about the job that lay ahead.

"It's going to be tough going on the beach," he said. "Somebody's going to get hurt."

FRIDAY, JULY 31, 1942

Today was a day of planning. Orders were being drawn up for everyone involved in the landing, from the majors and lieutenant colonels down to the buck privates.

Captain Gordon Gale, brilliant young executive officer of the Fifth Marines, talked about these plans to the officers before lunch in the wardroom. There were maps on one wall of the wardroom, behind the blackboard, showing the coasts of Guadalcanal and the beachhead we are to take. There was no map of Tulagi, the other first objective of the marines. I inquired and found that Tulagi is to be taken by the Marine Raiders, with other troops in support.

But the largest group of troops will concern

themselves solely with Guadalcanal. For that, it seems, is believed to be the most heavily fortified, most heavily occupied of the Japanese positions in the Solomons. And it contains a much-prized airfield that the Japanese have just about finished building.

In the afternoon I watched a group of marines cleaning and setting up their mortars and light machine guns on the forward deck. The lads were taking almost motherly care of the weapons. And I could see that the working parts were so well cleaned and oiled that they worked like the wheels of a watch that is in good running order.

Some of the men were sharpening bayonets, and indeed this seemed to be a popular pastime all over the ship. I saw one lad with a huge bolo knife, which he was carefully sharpening. Others worked at cleaning and oiling their rifles and submachine guns. Some of the boys had fashioned homemade blackjacks (canvas sacks containing lead balls) for "infighting."

"Is it true that the Japanese put gray paint on their faces, put some red stuff beside their mouths, and lie down and play dead until you pass 'em?" one fellow asked me.

I said I didn't know.

"Well, if they do," he said, "I'll stick 'em first."

20

Tonight at supper we talked about the pro-jected "softening up" of Guadalcanal by army B-17's. There's a rumor that the bombing should be starting tomorrow morning. We don't know the exact date on which we'll make our landing, but figure it should be within a week or so. And the "softening" process should last about a week.

SATURDAY, AUGUST 1, 1942
I stopped to talk to Lieutenant Snell (Evard J. Snell of Vineland, New Jersey), who is in charge of much of the paperwork involved in this effort. He estimated that probably only one out of every three boats will reach the shore in our attack attempt. As he explained, we will probably be faced by very strong forces, and only three out of four of us will survive the assault. That was his estimate.

When I saw the memorandum that had been prepared on the terrain we are to take, I could understand his high estimate of casualties.

It does not sound like an easy or safe terrain through which to advance. This impression was confirmed at a meeting for platoon leaders in the wardroom this afternoon. Lieutenant Colonel Maxwell, commanding officer of a battalion of assault troops, presided.

"This is going to be a difficult matter," he

said, "with the rivers to cross, the grass four to five feet tall, and the drainage ditches.

"But it can be done and it must be done, and we've got to lead the way. It's the first time in history we've ever had a huge expedition of this kind accompanied by transports. It's of worldwide importance. You'd be surprised if you knew how many people all over the world are following this. You cannot fail them."

MONDAY, AUGUST 3, 1942

Colonel Hunt issued a mimeographed notice to his troops this afternoon. "The coming offensive in the Guadalcanal area," he wrote, "marks the first offensive of the war against the enemy, involving ground forces of the United States. The marines have been selected to initiate this action which will prove to be the forerunner of successive offensive actions that will end in ultimate victory for our cause. Our country expects nothing but victory from us and it shall have just that. The word failure shall not even be considered as being in our vocabulary.

"We have worked hard and trained faithfully for this action, and I have every confidence in our ability and desire to force our will upon the enemy. We are meeting a tough and wily opponent, but he is not sufficiently tough or wily to overcome us because We Are Marines. [The capitals were the colonel's.]

"Our commanding general and staff are counting upon us and will give us wholehearted support and assistance. Our contemporaries of the other Task Organizations are red-blooded marines like ourselves and are ably led. They too will be there at the final downfall of the enemy.

"Each of us has his assigned task. Let each vow to perform it to the utmost of his ability, with added effort for good measure.

"Good luck and God bless you."

WEDNESDAY, AUGUST 5, 1942

"Scuttlebutt"—the navy and marine name for unfounded rumor—was rampant today. Naturally it would be, for we are riding up to the climax of our expedition.

One story was that one of our accompanying cruisers had found and sunk a Japanese submarine traveling on the surface. A marine told me he had seen the flashes of gunfire himself. I checked the story with the ship's executive officer. He laughed. "There was some heat lightning early this morning," he said, "behind that cruiser."

Another story told how we had discovered a lifeboat full of survivors. These were supposed

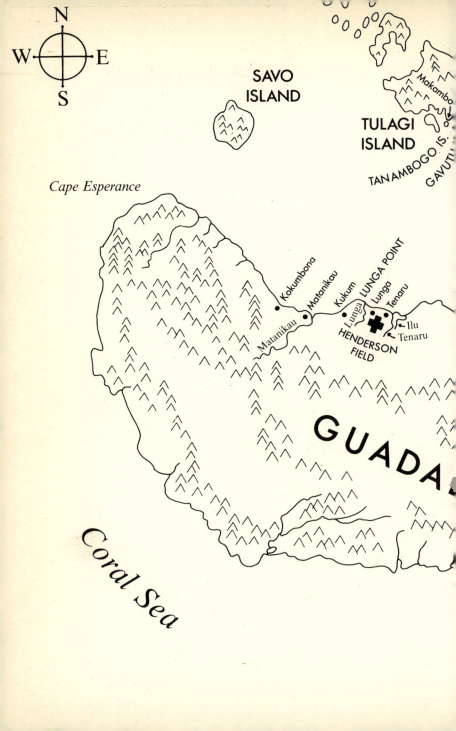

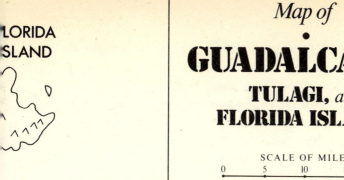

Map of
GUADALCANAL,
TULAGI, *and*
FLORIDA ISLANDS

SCALE OF MILES

0   5   10   15   20

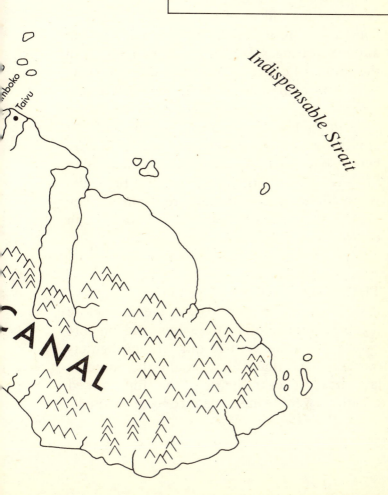

FLORIDA
ISLAND

Indispensable Strait

mboko

Taivu

CANAL

to be the remnant of the crew of sailors from a merchant ship that had been sunk by a Japanese destroyer. This story was equally easy to track down. It originated this morning, when our task force slowed for a few minutes for a motor whaleboat that was carrying dispatches from one transport to another.

In the cabin I found Captain Bill Hawkins, commanding officer of one of the two assault companies, busily oiling his submachine gun and his cartridges. He did not seem nervous. In the course of conversation I asked him how he felt about being one of the leaders of the first wave.

"I don't feel funny about it," he said. "I don't feel any more nervous than if I were being sent out to do a tough job in civilian life—you know, like trying to sell a big order when there's a lot of sales resistance." The captain had once sold groceries, wholesale, in Boston.

THURSDAY, AUGUST 6, 1942
It was easy to see that this was the day before the big event. Sailors were busy rigging big booms to the heaviest of our landing lighters (barges), so that they could be quickly launched. At several parts of the ship, canned C-rations were being issued: concentrated cof-

26

fee and biscuits, meat and beans, vegetable stew, and D-ration chocolate bars—enough for two or three days' subsistence until field kitchens can be rigged on Guadalcanal.

In the ship's armorer's shop was a crowd of officers and men working single-mindedly at the benches, giving their weapons a last-minute check of adjustment. I picked up a .45-caliber automatic. I knew that on the island the Japanese weren't going to ask whether I was a correspondent before they started to shoot. In the jungle I would look like any other marine.

We all wondered at the fact that our task force, now well within range of the Japanese, had not been attacked by submarine, plane, or surface craft. But there was not even an alarm.

The weather has been greatly in our favor. All day today there was a heavy overcast, and visibility was very limited. Unless the Japanese had come very close, they could not have spotted us. Still, we were amazed, and I for one wondered if they might have prepared a trap for us to walk into.

It was announced tonight that breakfast will be served at 4:30 a.m. We will reach our launching point at about 6:20. The zero hour has not yet been set, but it will be somewhere near 8:30.

After dinner I talked to Colonel Hunt, in whose assault boat I will be going ashore. He

27

said that Colonel Maxwell and some of the other officers will be going in another boat. "No use putting all your eggs in one basket," he said, and that had an uncomfortably hazardous sound.

· 4 ·
LANDING

FRIDAY, AUGUST 7, 1942

It was no trouble to get up at four o'clock this morning without benefit of an alarm clock, for my mind had been trained for this day for a long time.

Everyone was calm at breakfast. We knew we must be very near our objective by this time, probably at that moment passing directly under the Japanese shore guns. And the fact that we had got this far without any action made us feel strangely secure, as if getting up at four o'clock in the morning and preparing to force a landing on the enemy shore were perfectly normal things to do on an August morning in the South Seas. We had a heavy

29

breakfast and carried on a normally humorous conversation.

Up on deck the situation was the same. Everyone seemed ready to jump at the first boom of a gun, but there was little excitement. The thing that was happening was so unbelievable that it seemed like a dream. We were slipping through the narrow neck of water between Guadalcanal and Savo Island; we were practically inside Tulagi Bay, almost past the Japanese shore batteries, and not a shot had been fired.

On deck, marines lined the starboard rail, straining their eyes and pointing their field glasses toward the high, irregular dark mass that lay beyond the silently moving shapes that were our accompanying ships. The land mass was Guadalcanal Island. The sky was still dark; as yet there was no predawn glow, but the rugged black mountains stood quite distinct against the lighter sky.

There was not much talking among the usually lively marines. The only sounds were the swish of water around our ship, the slight noises of men moving about on the forward deck.

Up on the bridge I found the ship's officers less calm than the marines. Theirs was the worry of getting the ship to anchorage without her being sunk, and they seemed high-strung and incredulous.

"I can't believe it," one lieutenant said to me. "I wonder if the Japanese can be that dumb. Either they're very dumb, or it's a trick."

But there was no sign of any trick as we plowed on into the bay. The sky began to throw light ahead of us, and we could even see the misty outline of Tulagi and the Florida group of islands squatting to the east and north.

Now the rugged mass of Guadalcanal Island was growing more distinct, and the sharp shoulders of the high mountains could be seen. But there was no sign of any firing from shore, nor were any enemy planes spotted.

Suddenly, from the bridge, I saw a brilliant yellow-green flash of light coming from the gray shape of a cruiser on our starboard bow. Red pencil lines of shells arched through the sky, and I saw flashes on the dark shore of Guadalcanal where they struck. A second later I heard the *b-rroom-boom* of the cannonading. I should have been ready for that, but I was so nervous that I jumped at the sound.

Our naval barrage, which was to pave the way for our landing, had begun. I looked at my watch. The time was 6:14.

31

Two minutes later a cruiser astern and to our starboard side began firing. There were the same greenish-yellow flashes as the salvo went off, the same red rockets arching across the sky, geysers of red fires where the shells struck shore, and the terrifying rumble and boom of the explosion.

Now, fore and aft, the two cruisers were hurling salvo after salvo into the Guadalcanal shore. It was fascinating to watch the apparent slowness with which the shells curved through the air. Distance, of course, caused that apparent slowness. But despite the distance, the concussion of the firing shook the deck of our ship and stirred our trouser legs with sudden gusts of wind.

At 6:17 a sheaf of tracer bullets showered from the bay in toward shore, and simultaneously we heard the sound of plane motors. Our planes were strafing, we knew, though in the half-light we could not make out the shapes of the aircraft.

At 6:19 another cruiser, dead ahead of us, began firing. A moment later other warships joined, and the flash of their firing and the arcs of their flying shells illuminated the sky.

Other ships of our force—the group under General Rupertus—had turned to the left toward Tulagi, and heavy reports of cannonading were coming from them too.

At 6:28 I noticed a brilliant white spot of fire on the water ahead and watched, fascinated, while it burgeoned into a spreading sheet of red flame. Planes were moving back and forth over the spot like flies.

"It's a Japanese ship," said the ship's officer standing next to me. His field glasses were leveled on the flames. "Planes did it," he said. "They were strafing."

The sheet of red flame crept out into a long, thin line, and then it mounted higher and higher into a sort of low-slung, fiery pyramid. For long minutes we watched the flames while the din of our thundering naval guns increased and reached a climax around us.

Ahead of us, to the left of the still brightly burning Japanese ship, I saw a bright, white pinpoint of light blink into existence. It was a masthead light riding atop the Australian cruiser* that had led our procession into the bay.

Our ship was still moving forward, however, and the flaming ship ahead was growing nearer. In the light of the red-orange flames we could see that it was not a large craft and that it was low in the water. Possibly it was 120 feet long.

* The *Canberra*, sunk in subsequent naval action in the Solomon Islands area.

"What kind of a ship is it?" I asked a deck officer.

"They say it's a torpedo boat," he said.

But it turned out to be a schooner that had been carrying a load of oil and gasoline. That accounted for the flames.

Our dive-bombers were swooping low over the beach. In the growing daylight we could see the color of the explosions where bombs were landing. Some, which struck at the edge of the water, had a bluish tinge. Others, hitting farther back in the sand and earth, were darker.

As the planes dived they were strafing. The incandescent lines of their tracers struck into the ground, then bent back, ricocheting toward the sky to form the now-familiar shallow V.

Our ship and one other, the vanguard of the transport fleet, slowed and stopped. Immediately the davits began to clank as the boats were lowered away. There was a hubbub of shouts and the sound of many men moving about the ship. On the forward deck a donkey engine began to chuff and puff. The time had come for the beginning of our landing adventure.

It was daylight, but ahead the mass of flames that was the burning Japanese boat glowed as brightly as in the dark of the night. As we watched, there were new explosions within the fire—probably gasoline tanks. A burning oil slick spread across the water astern of the boat. And the thought crossed my mind that if there had been anyone alive aboard that craft, he certainly was not alive now.

Our accompanying cruisers, which had stopped firing for a few moments, were opening up again. One, lying astern and to our starboard side, was sending salvo after salvo into a dark point of land. A column of dense black smoke was rising from the spot where the shells were landing. And as we watched, the base of the column glowed red and orange, and the boom of a distant explosion came to us.

I walked among the troops gathered on the forward deck and found them silent and nervous. Gone were the gaiety and song of the few preceding days. There did not seem to be much to say, although a few lads came up to me with the inevitable remark, "Well, this is it."

The first of our marines clambered over the rail and swung down the rope nets into the boats. As these pulled away, more boats came up, and the seeping waterfall of marines continued to slide over the side.

I got word that it was time for me to debark. I took one last look around the ship. Toward the shore of Guadalcanal I could see the cruisers still pasting shells into the landscape. On

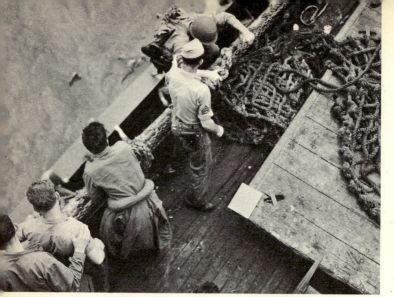

A marine goes over the side to be taken to Guadalcanal.

With guns poised for action, amphibian tractors swiftly carry marines to the shores of Guadalcanal.

the point of land, Kukum, where the bombardment had set a fuel dump afire, there was a new fire now: two columns of smoke instead of one. From Tulagi, across the bay, one could hear the sounds of heavy cannonading. The landing must be going ahead there.

It was just eight o'clock when I hit the deck of the bobbing landing boat. Colonel Hunt and his staff officers were already aboard. This was to be a "free" boat; the colonel could take it ashore at any time he pleased. He might go in after the first landing wave, and at any rate we would not be later than the fifth wave.

At 8:06 a covering screen of fighter planes appeared and flew over the fleet of transports. They shuttled back and forth overhead, weaving a protective net in the sky.

For a long time our landing boat circled astern of our ship while we sat in the bottom, keeping our heads below the gunwale in the approved fashion.

At 8:34 the navy coxswain swung our boat around and we headed for shore. We were moving slowly, however, throttled back.

Kneeling so that I could look over the gunwale, I saw that our warships had ceased firing for the time being. From Tulagi in the north, however, came the sound of heavy cannonading.

At 9:02 our boat was moving toward the

beach at full throttle when the line of cruisers and destroyers ahead of us began a terrific bombardment of the shore. This was the "softener" that would, we hoped, sweep the beach clean of any Japanese machine gun or artillery emplacements and make our landing easier.

Scores of naval guns blasted simultaneously into the shore. The din of their firing was intense. Sheets of yellow flame welled from the gun barrels up and down the line, and along the beach a line of blue and black geysers leaped up where the shells were striking.

At 9:05 the intense bombardment on the shore was ending. A haze of dirty black smoke hung over the edge of the land. And we were heading straight for it.

We followed, not too distantly, the first wave of landing boats, which we could see as an irregular line of moving white spots against the blue water, each spot dotted at the center with black. The white spots, we knew, were foam; the black spots were the boats themselves, making maximum speed toward shore.

We could not see the boats strike shore, but signals rose ahead of us on the beach. The colonel turned to the rest of us in the boat and smiled. That smile was the agreed signal for a successful landing. A signalman stood on our motor hatch and wigwagged the good news back to our mother ship. It was quickly acknowledged.

The fact of a successful landing, however, did not mean that taking the beachhead would be easy. The enemy might open fire, so we ducked well below the level of the gunwales when we were a certain number of yards from shore.

At 9:28 we passed the boats of the first wave, coming out from the beach to the ships to get another load of troops. We poked our heads up and saw that they showed no signs of having been damaged by enemy fire. We gathered a little more courage now and raised our heads higher to see what was happening. Lieutenant Cory, squatting next to me, shouted to me over the rumble of the motor that perhaps there were no Japanese. Still, it seemed that this would be too good to be true. Perhaps they were merely drawing us into a trap.

At 9:40 we were close enough to land to see isolated palm trees projecting above the shore—a sign that we were coming close to whatever trap the enemy might have prepared.

In our boat there was no talking, despite the excitement of the moment. The motor was making too much noise, at any rate. We sat and looked at each other and occasionally peeped over the side to glimpse other boats plunging shoreward, or to cock an eye at the strangely silent beach.

At 9:47 we were close enough to the shore to see a long line of our landing boats drawn up on the dun-colored sand. A wallowing tank moved along the shoreline, tossing plumes of spray before and behind. We could make out throngs of our troops moving on the beach among a line of thatched huts. We then became very courageous, since it was apparent that there were no enemy troops in the vicinity.

At 9:50, with a jolt, our boat grounded on the beach. Our debarkation was leisurely. I jumped carefully from the bow and got only one foot wet, and that slightly. It was hardly the hell-for-leather leap and dash through the surf, with the accompaniment of rattling machine guns, that I had expected.

From down the beach a jeep, evidently the first ashore, came past us. There was noise and motion everywhere as more troops leaped from beached landing boats, and working parties struggled to unload bigger barges coming in with machinery, equipment, and supplies.

A group of five fighter planes zoomed close overhead. A tractor was being hauled from a tank lighter (a barge). I saw two marines setting up a small generator between two bamboo huts that had been badly damaged by the shell fire. The generator would run a radio.

40

I attempted to discover if any opposition had been encountered. "I heard machine gun firing when I came in," said one marine, "but I don't know whether it was ours or the enemy's."

"There's a little firing in there," said another marine, motioning toward the jungle. "Looks like the Japanese will take to the hills."

At 10:20 a procession of jeeps towing carts of shells moved through the coconut trees and out toward our forward positions. The procession was a reminder that deep inland our troops might at that moment be tangling with the Japanese.

But there were no sounds of cannonading coming from inland. Only from the direction of Tulagi, twenty miles to the north, could we hear the boom of distant cannon fire.

Back on the beach the activity of peaceful unloading continued. The sand was now torn and rutted by the constant traffic of jeeps and tractors. Our first tank was being pulled from a lighter. Anti-aircraft guns were being rolled out and set up on the beach, their barrels pointing seaward.

A medical-aid station had been set up on the sand under a Red Cross banner. The attending medico, Dr. C. Douglas Hoyt, said that there had been no casualties so far, except for a lad who cut his palm with a machete while trying to open a coconut. That was cheerful news.

By this time fast-moving Colonel Hunt had disappeared from the beach, taking his staff with him. I set out to overtake him, using as a guide his command post telephone lines, which it seemed had sprung through the conquered terrain almost instantaneously.

I passed through the coastal belt of coconut palms, then through a beaten path cutting through a field of shoulder-high parched grass, and then into the thick, shadowy jungle. There, fortunately, a trail had been cut.

I found Colonel Hunt's command post, as it was called, actually only an undistinguished part of the jungle, where communications men were busy installing field telephones. It was time for lunch. We squatted in the matting of soft, wet leaves and opened ration cans.

Things were quite peaceful. The colonel said that apparently no resistance had been encountered by our landing party. If there were any Japanese about, they had faded into the hills. Captain Charles V. Hodgess, one of our Australian guides and the former owner of a coconut plantation on Guadalcanal, joked about the ease with which we had occupied Guadalcanal thus far. "I'm exhausted by the arduousness of landing against such heavy fire," he said.

I went back to the jungle, headed for the col-

Marine commanders in a picture taken four days after the landing on Guadalcanal. Shown are most of the officers who led the First Marine Division.

onel's advance party—and missed the first Japanese air raid on the marines at Guadalcanal.

At 1:30 I heard the quick, low *whoomp, whoomp, whoomp* of anti-aircraft fire and saw the sky fill with the dark brown smudges of shell bursts. The sky was overcast, and there were no planes visible, but the droning of motors could be heard. It was evident that the Japanese were after the transports and warships in the bay, for the anti-aircraft bursts

43

were concentrated over that area. Trees then blocked my view of the ships, but I was to learn later in the day that they had not been hit.

At about 1:40 the sound of anti-aircraft firing stopped. A few moments after that, eighteen of our carrier-based fighter planes swung out of the overcast sky and swept across Tulagi Bay. Evidently the air raid was over.

I caught up with the colonel's party in the woods and plowed steadily along with them through jungle trails. Just before four o'clock we reached a pleasant coconut grove. We had just sat down to rest our bones when a terrific concentration of anti-aircraft fire could be heard breaking, and again the bursts were visible in the sky.

The command "Take cover" was passed, and we slid for the bush, wondering if the Japanese would come in and strafe our troops. But this time, like the time before, their target was evidently the ships. The anti-aircraft fire lasted five minutes. We neither heard the bombs nor saw the planes. Then the raid was over. It had been as tame as our landing. (But I was later to find out that for the ships involved, the raid had been furious. Japanese dive-bombers had attacked our warships, damaging one. Two of the attackers had been shot down by anti-aircraft fire.)

44

In the coconut grove it was strange to see a marine pick up a telephone and hear him say "Operator" into the receiver. It seemed strange, too, to hear French horns, sounding exactly like those you might find on a fashionable roadster, tooting in the jungle. It happened that they were attached to the tanks.

"I'll be right out," said a marine after one such toot. It was as if his girl were waiting outside in a new convertible.

There was an end even to this amusement. We had to get up and march again for miles through the jungle, through coconut groves, across boggy streams, and over steep little hills.

At 4:30 we came out of the trees to an open field of tall grass. Two marines stood at the edge of the field. They had their .45 automatics in their hands and seemed a little nervous. One of them approached the colonel.

"We found fresh-chopped trees that looked like they'd been cut about an hour ago, sir," he said. "We think it was a Japanese gun emplacement."

But half an hour later, after some more painful trudging under heavy packs, we had not seen any signs of the enemy. We halted, then, in a grove of white coconut palms that must have been beautiful when it was well kept. Now there were piles of decaying palm fronds and aged, rotting coconuts on the ground, but we settled down to rest without a murmur of complaint. Anything would have looked like home after the day's hiking.

We had a canned ration supper and, since there was no water, many of the lads busied themselves with knocking down green coconuts from the trees and cutting them open for milk.

Bedding down for the night under the tall palms and a covering of soft stars would have been a beautiful experience, except for bugs, mosquitoes, and thirst—which unfortunately were all too present.

With the coming of the dark, the macaws began to squeal in the treetops, and rifle shots became more numerous. The sentries were jittery on this first night on the island.

I awoke from time to time to hear the call of "Halt!" followed almost immediately by volleys of gunfire.

Once, near midnight, I heard a submachine gun cracking very near the grove. Then a rifle barked. Then another. And soon five or six guns were firing simultaneously, and the bright tracer bullets were zipping in several directions over the grove where we lay. Some of the slugs whined through the trees close by. Then the firing fell off and died, and we went back to sleep again.

SATURDAY, AUGUST 8, 1942

A runner came back this morning to report that the airport, prize of the Guadalcanal invasion, has been reached and that, as yet, no contact has been made with the enemy.

But one of our sentries, who had a post last night at the outskirts of our coconut grove, said that near daybreak a patrol of about 150 Japanese passed close by our bivouac and then took off into the bush.

Colonel Hunt pointed up the moral. "This is no picnic," he said, obviously concerned over the fact that we have had an easy time of the campaign thus far. "We've got to be careful."

The colonel set his helmet on the ground, sat down on it, and unfolded a map. His staff, gathered around for the day's orders, stood by, watching.

"I'll tell you what I know and then you'll know as much as I do," the colonel said. He pointed a big finger at a spot on the map. "Here's where we are. We've got to work down there and get to the Tenaru. Probably we'll wade around the mouth of the river." He went into the details of our plans.

The colonel passed along the good news that operations on Tulagi and Gavutu, across the bay, were going well. Tulagi, assaulted by the Raiders, was okay despite heavy resistance.

The troops, attacking the neighboring island of Gavutu, had "taken their first objective and the rest is in the bag."

We trudged along through the jungle for miles, reached and forded the river, passed through another coconut grove, scared up a herd of horses, and came out on the beach again—without seeing a single Japanese.

We passed through a little village of tin-roofed huts on the beach. The white-plastered walls had been shot through and in some cases shattered by the naval gunfire. The roofs had been turned into sieves by flying H.E. (high explosive) fragments.

Evidently these huts had been used as barracks by the Japanese troops, for there were signs on the walls bearing Japanese inscriptions. I took one to Lieutenant Cory, the interpreter. "It says Unit Number Three," he said, "in charge of so-and-so."

Sailors are amazingly efficient souvenir hunters. I saw some of them here with our advance units; they were busy collecting the Japanese signs.

I stopped to talk with Colonel Frank B. Goettge, the division intelligence officer. He suggested that the Japanese would probably be in today to try another attack on the transports, which still lay close offshore. So, when Colonel Hunt's people cut from the beach back into the jungle, I stayed behind on the shore—and saw one of the most awe-inspiring spectacles I have ever witnessed.

It was just noon when the quick-paced *whoomp-whoomp* of anti-aircraft firing began. I could see black bursts plastering the dome of the sky over Tulagi and the flash of gunfire coming from the Australian cruiser out in the bay. Then the other warships took it up, and the whooping sounds came in overlapping clusters and volleys. Overhead, the canopy of anti-aircraft bursts was spreading thicker and farther over the sky.

Then to the thunder of the big anti-aircraft guns was added the fierce rattling of smaller anti-aircraft guns. The whole sound swelled until it seemed to swarm into your ears. Suddenly I saw the first Japanese plane moving in among the transports. Like a preying shark, it was skimming over the water below the level of the masts, and I thought "Torpedo plane!"

Now I could see other Japanese planes prowling low over the water, darting among the transports. And there were black spouts of water rising amidst them: these must have been the splashes of ack-ack (anti-aircraft fire), or perhaps torpedoes being launched by the enemy aircraft.

The ships were moving over the horizon now, racing for the narrow straits that led to

the open sea. They were trying to get out before they were hit.

Our fighter planes dived into the foray. I saw
one of them rout a Japanese plane out of the
fracas and chase it fiercely, with the enemy
plane apparently in panicky flight toward the
western tip of Guadalcanal. I heard the popping and rattling of our plane's machine guns,
continuing for seconds on end. Suddenly the
Japanese plane began to trail smoke. Then fire
came at the root of the smoke plume, and the
plane, falling, traced a steadily brightening
curve across the sky. I watched, fascinated,
while the aircraft arched into the water, and
the slow white fountain of a great splash rose
behind it. Then the white splash turned into
brilliant orange as the plane exploded and sent
a sheet of flame backfiring a hundred feet into
the sky.

I turned my field glasses back to the fleet in
time to see a huge flash of fire burst along the
upper deck of one of the transports, the *George
F. Elliott*. Then a clump of sooty black smoke
billowed out from the blood-red roots and
towered up into the sky. The transport must
have been hit directly. (I found out later that
one of the Japanese planes had crashed, apparently by accident, into the ship just aft of
the bridge.)

Almost at the same time, three other columns of smoke arose just over the rim of the horizon. I surmised that other ships had been hit.

The panorama of action stretched all the way from east to west. I had seen one Japanese plane fall in flames far to the left. Now, to the right, two others were falling in clouds of smoke.

In the center of the picture the stricken transport was still burning. The red flames mounted into the smoke, spreading belches of fire high up into the clouds as an explosion occurred.

But suddenly the sky was empty of Japanese planes. The awful storm of firing had stopped. The raid was over. I looked at my watch. It was 12:10.

At 12:54 the transports had turned and were moving to their anchorage off our beach. But out in the middle of the bay, the badly hit *Elliott* was still burning, with her fires evidently out of control. (Later she was abandoned and scuttled.)

A marine, passing by, told me he had counted six of the Japanese planes falling. (I found out later that there had been forty Japanese planes attacking; that sixteen of these were shot down on the spot, and the remaining twenty-four destroyed by our fighters, one by one, as they streaked for home. The Japanese

torpedo bombers had not gone after the war-ships, contenting themselves with merely straf-ing the transports as they passed by.)

I started back inland, to catch up again with the marine forces making their way toward the airfield. At 1:30 I passed two marines bringing in the first Japanese prisoners.

There were three of them, walking in single file, and the marines, looking huge by com-parison, shooed them along like pigeons.

The prisoners were a measly lot. None of them was more than five feet tall, and they were puny. Their skin was sallow. The first two in line had shaved heads and were bare from the waist down; the marines had been diligent in their search for weapons.

The third had been allowed to keep his khaki-colored trousers. He wore a scraggly beard that made him look even more wretched, and on his head he had a visored cap of cheap cloth with a cloth anchor insignia.

The prisoners blinked their eyes like curious birds as they looked at me. The first in line gaped, a gold tooth very prominent in the cen-ter of his open mouth.

To one side of the road rested three Japa-nese trucks. Freshly painted in gray, and seemingly in first-class condition, they looked like the latest American models.

Across the road sat a Ford V8 sedan, camouflaged in green and carrying Japanese navy license plates. It was apparently an officer's car.

When we entered the Japanese tent camp, we knew why we had been able to sail into Tulagi Bay and under enemy guns without being fired upon. The enemy had been caught completely unaware.

In the first of the big tents—there were scores of them—we burst in upon a breakfast table left in a rush. It looked as if the Japanese had run out the back door as we came in the front.

Serving dishes, set in the middle of the table, were filled with meat stew, rice, and cooked prunes. Bowls and saucers around the edge were half full of food. Chopsticks had been left propped on the edges of dishes, or dropped in haste on the floor mat.

In other tents we found more signs that the Japanese had run in panicky surprise when our assault began. Shoes, mosquito nets, toilet articles, soap, and other essentials had been left behind.

As we walked on through Japanese territory that afternoon, we began to realize the huge quantities of booty we had fallen heir to. I passed the buildings of the airfield, the big prize of our expedition. The Japanese had a radar installation there, although we had thought they didn't know about radar. The coral-surfaced landing strip was now completely occupied by our troops. I saw rows of brand-new wooden barracks—so new that the Japanese had not yet moved in.

I climbed aboard a tank and rode to Lunga Point. There we found a large enemy camp and great quantities of equipment.

We rode past a large gray frame house which I was told contained a Japanese electrical plant. We passed through a grove where our shells had torn half the trees asunder, and came to a huge motor-transport dump, complete with repair shop. Here were at least a hundred Japanese trucks.

Beyond the truck dump we came to a great camp of tents, the largest we had yet seen. Then, at a beautiful bend in the river, we saw the buildings that had evidently been the Japanese headquarters. Here were shacks that contained iron beds (most of the acres of surrounding tents had only board platforms topped with mats), handsome French telephone receivers, radios, and riding boots standing in corners.

The house that had evidently been occupied by the commanding officer was well stocked with luxuries such as bottles of wine and a large radio set. Nearby stood a bathtub, the crowning luxury on this hot tropical island.

Along the road in front of Japanese head-

A Japanese supply shack, captured by marines, yields everything from candy to heavy machinery.

Former Japanese barracks serve as a hospital for American troops.

quarters was a long line of our own trucks and jeeps, moving personnel and supplies forward. A captured Japanese car was in the procession. On the other side of the road, in the truck dump, marines were trying to start up the Japanese vehicles. Most of them, it seemed, were ready to go except that the ignition keys were missing.

Few of our troops had investigated one Japanese building with open sidewalls. I wandered in and found a large drafting table equipped with properly up-angled drawing boards in the center of the building, and a desk on a sort of porch at one end. Around the edge of the room were shelves filled with blueprints, drafting supplies, stocks of paper, and record books. This must have been the headquarters office.

One of the drafting boards had half-finished plans, drawn on tissue paper, pinned to it. The drafting pen lay across the center of the drawing, evidence of a helter-skelter withdrawal. Nearby a French phone lay beside its receiver—as if a conversation had been interrupted by our arrival.

·5·
CONTACT

SUNDAY, AUGUST 9, 1942

A little after midnight this morning, the rain began to pour down on Guadalcanal.

I had just dropped off to sleep when I awoke to find people whispering and heard the *brroom-brroom-brroom* of cannonading coming from the sea.

It had stopped raining. We stood in a quiet group under the palms, listening and watching. Flashes of gunfire were filling the sky, and a few seconds after each flash we could hear the booming of the guns that had caused it.

The salvos of firing came with increased intensity. Then, for a few moments, the flashes and the booming stopped and the sky was quiet. Then the cannonading began again, seeming louder, brighter, and closer than before.

We knew then that a sea fight was going on. Possibly it was the battle for Guadalcanal. Possibly, if our people out there lost the battle, the Japanese would be ashore before morning, and we would have to fight for our lives. We knew that the fate of all of us hung on that sea battle. In that moment I realized how much we must depend on ships even in our land operations. And in that moment I think most of us who were there watching the gunfire suddenly knew the awful feeling of being pitifully small, knew for a moment that we were only tiny particles caught up in the gigantic whirlpool of war.

At about 2:30 some of the men said they were sure the sound of cannonading was growing fainter, and that this meant the Japanese were being driven back. At three o'clock the last barrage came to an end.

I sought refuge this time in a Japanese sedan, probably a commander's vehicle, which had been left at the side of the road. The soft cushions felt good. Except for the slight disturbance of being bitten by mosquitoes, I was quite comfortable the rest of the night.

This morning I made a trek to the temporary command post of General Vandegrift (Major

General Alexander A. Vandegrift of Washington, D.C., and Lynchburg, Virginia). The general, a red-cheeked, exceedingly affable man, told me that the casualties on Tulagi and Gavutu have not been so heavy as at first estimated. On both islands the Japanese holed themselves up in caves and dugouts, he said, and fought to the last man. The conquest of Tanambogo was complete, he said, and today the smaller island, Makambo, was being taken. The marines also had a second foothold on the largest island across the bay, called Florida or N'Gela. That was good news. But there was no news as yet about what happened in the sea battle to the northwest this morning.

General Alexander A. Vandegrift (left) served as commander of the First Marine Division during most of the Guadalcanal campaign.

MONDAY, AUGUST 10, 1942

This morning I went to Kukum, on our western flank, to join a patrol of marines. The plan was to probe still farther west to try to discover if there were enemy troops out there. Kukum, I found, was a group of tin-roofed shacks along the coast, with a few little piers built out into the water. The shacks had been severely damaged by our shelling; there was scarcely a wall that was not pocked by H.E. fragments.

We watched the trees carefully as we moved out of the bivouac area and started down the coast, keeping about a quarter of a mile inland so as to avoid being seen by the enemy during our approach to the neighboring village of Matanikau.

We saw no Japanese for some hours, although there were several false alarms. At about 9:30 a runner appeared from one of our flanking platoons as we halted for a rest. "Captain," he said to Captain Kaempfer, "there are some Japanese over to our left rear." At the word, our men scattered and took cover. But no Japanese turned up.

At 11:40 we were working our way down the beach at the fringe of the jungle when there came a sudden spattering of sharp rifle reports to our left and ahead. Deeper-toned rifles took up the chorus, machine guns joined in, and the shower of sound became a rainstorm. What had happened was that Japanese riflemen and machine gunners had opened up on our left flank, and our own rifles, submachine guns, and machine guns were returning the fire.

The sound of firing was coming from farther down the beach, too, and it took me only a second or two to flop down amid a row of marines who had taken cover behind a long white log.

We lay there a few minutes while the marines fired down the beach and into the jungle on the left. Then I noticed that all of our lads had pulled their heads way down and were lying extremely flat on the sand. In a minute I knew the reason. A marine on the far end of the log had been hit; he was holding one hand over the lower part of his face.

"Corpsman!" somebody shouted. "Pass the word back for a corpsman. We've got a wounded man here!"

There was a lull in the firing. I scrambled for the jungle fringe and worked my way back to the trail. I had just reached the edge of it when another volley of firing broke out ahead of me. Again I heard the shout: "Pass the word back for a corpsman."

Now the trail was fairly well filled with marines. And so the Japanese began to fire again.

We took cover before the Japanese could score any hits. I crouched amidst some sharp-edged pineapple plants behind a tree. But the enemy was firing from our rear now. Evidently there were snipers in the trees back there. It was hard to take cover under the circumstances.

I heard a bullet go *phffft* over my head, and another plop into the underbrush beside me. I moved into a denser part of the jungle—quickly.

Then the firing stopped. Our officers held a hasty council of war, and it was decided to return to Kukum. So, sending our wounded back on a jeep, we made the long, tedious trek back to base.

At Kukum we heard scuttlebutt about the great sea battle that was fought yesterday on the northwest of Guadalcanal, near Savo Island. In that battle, which had kept us awake and worried through much of the early morning, five of our cruisers had been lost, according to the rumor. Five Japanese cruisers had also been sunk. That was the story. There was no official word on the matter at Marine Corps headquarters except the announcement that the Australian cruiser *Canberra* had been sunk.

(Later it was learned that we had lost four cruisers in the battle during the early hours yesterday morning. Those were the *Canberra,* the *Astoria,* the *Vincennes,* and the *Quincy.* The enemy lost no ships.)

TUESDAY, AUGUST 11, 1942

It was a quiet day. The bad news about our cruisers depressed us. We knew now that the Battle of Savo was a bad defeat. Our position here seems unprotected. Some are saying this will be another Bataan. But we heard from Tulagi that all objectives there had been attained—except for isolated snipers. Bob Miller, the only other news correspondent on the island, and I made arrangements to go to Tulagi tomorrow.

WEDNESDAY, AUGUST 12, 1942

We were down at the beach early this morning. And after considerable delay we finally boarded the small fleet of three motorboats that were to take us to Tulagi. Two of the craft were the regulation type of landing boat. The third was a tank lighter filled with drums of gasoline. For armament we had .30-caliber guns on the landing boats and .50-caliber guns on the lighter.

As we set out in the glaring sun, Marine Gunner Banta (Sheffield M. Banta of Staten Island, New York), who was in charge of our boat, warned our crew to keep an especially sharp lookout for airplanes. Also, he said, for submarines. But I could see that our crewmen spent most of their time anxiously watching

During a break, a marine cleans his rifle.

the sky, and that their principal worry was a strafing attack from the air. This turned out to be a mistake in judgment.

"I think that may be a submarine over there," said someone in the boat. And although we looked where he pointed, we did not believe we would actually see one.

But it *was* a submarine—a long, low black shape, with a rise at the center where the conning tower stood. It was a big Japanese fleet-type sub. He was moving away from us. But when we spotted him, he also spotted us. Slowly he swung around and headed so as to cross our bow.

He was now a mile or two ahead of us, to our

port side. We could see the line of white spray threading along the base of the slim black hull as he picked up speed. We were going to have a *race* on our hands. We knew that then, and I knew that I would not again scoff at the melodramatic formula of "Race for Life or Race with Death" as being improbable.

In our little boat there was confusion for a few moments as everybody shouted at once. There was some doubt as to what we should do. Should we run back to Guadalcanal or head for the open sea? Or would it be better to cut for the eastern, right-hand tip of Florida Island and try to reach it before the submarine

Relaxed marines line up for chow.

cut us off? There was no time for debate. Gunner Banta gave the order to head for Florida Island, and Coxswain Charles N. Stickney of Newbury, Michigan, swung our helm sharply to the right and opened the throttle.

Our boat began to jar and pound against the choppy waves as we suddenly picked up speed, and sheets of spray bowled over the bow and drenched us.

The other boats of our little fleet were also pounding along at full speed, tossing plumes of white spray over their cockpits.

But the submarine was gaining. It was evident that he was moving swiftly and that our race with him was going to be close. We might have to swim for it, even if we won the race. Through my field glasses, I saw small black figures of men run out on the sub's deck toward the long silhouette of her big gun.

This was one item I had not even considered—shellfire. It was a horrifying sight to see geysers of water leaping up between us and the submarine, for we knew then that he was ranging in on us. We heard the sharp bang of the shells exploding and knew they would soon be coming dangerously close.

Then there were more geysers, closer to the submarine, and we were mystified for a moment, until we heard the booming of gunfire coming from the Tulagi shore. We knew then, and were thankful, that a shore battery was opening up on the submarine.

But the shells were not yet falling near the sub. And each time he fired his gun, he ranged closer to us.

I tried to fix my field glasses on the submarine, but our boat jerked and bounced so, and the spray doused the lenses in such a steady downpour, that the attempt was futile.

Our clothes were soaking. I started to wrap my field glasses in my field jacket, then undid the bundle. No use trying to keep things dry. We were going to have to swim for it. I could see that. The submarine was gaining on us, and a shell landed only a hundred yards or so astern of us.

Just then we saw that the men in the other landing boat were waving wildly at us. One of the seamen had jumped up on the boat's hatch and was trying to send us a message by signal flag. A haze of smoke rose from the motor hatch of the other boat. We could see that it was in trouble. Our boat swung over next to the crippled one and we bumped gunwales, pulled apart, and smashed together again as the two boats, running at top speed, ran parallel courses.

The crew of the other craft fell, slid, and vaulted into our boat. Lieutenant Herb Merrillat (Herbert L. Merrillat of Monmouth, New

Jersey), a marine public relations officer and ordinarily a quite dignified young man, jumped over from the boat and landed, a disordered collection of arms and legs, on the bottom of our boat. He was wearing white socks. In his haste he had left his shoes behind. Even in that moment the sight of his descent was humorous.

But we had lost precious time in picking up the other crew. Now the submarine had gained a good lead and our fate seemed hopeless. I told myself that this was my last day of existence, as it seemed certain to be.

But the splashes of the shore batteries were coming closer to the submarine. We saw several that appeared to be only a few yards from the conning tower. And one of our crewmen shouted "Smoke! She's smoking!" I could not see any smoke. But it was plain that the shells were now beginning to come too close for the comfort of those in the submarine. For the sub was turning away from us and toward the open sea to the west. We had been saved in the nick of time. The ordeal was over.

We sailed into the calm waters of Tulagi harbor, down the narrow passage of water walled by greenery, and came to a small wooden dock. It was a distinct pleasure to set foot on land again.

We talked to Colonel Edson (Merritt A.

Edson of Chester, Vermont) commanding officer of the Marine Raiders, who had assaulted and taken Tulagi. He was a wiry man with a lean, hard face partly covered by a sparse, spiky growth of grayish beard. His light blue eyes were tired and red-rimmed in appearance, for he was weary now from long days of fighting, and his red eyebrows and eyelashes, being almost invisible, heightened the effect. But his eyes were cold as steel, and it was interesting to notice that even when he was being pleasant, they never smiled. He talked rapidly, spitting his words out like bullets, his hard-lipped mouth snapping shut like a trap. Hardly a creature of sunlight and air, he; but I could see that he was a first-class fighting man. (Colonel Edson later won two outstanding victories on Guadalcanal and was awarded the Navy Cross and the Congressional Medal of Honor.)

Colonel Edson summarized the Tulagi campaign. "The Japanese had one battalion, of about four hundred and fifty men, on the island," he said. "They were all troops—no laborers. All of their defenses were located on the southeast part of the island. Our landing was at eight fifteen a.m. on Friday, August seventh, at the northwest part. There were only small obstructionist groups out there.

"The Japanese casualties were about four hundred. Not a single one gave up. One prisoner was taken; he had been dazed by a close mortar burst. When a man went in one of the holes to get the radio, he found seventeen dead Japanese. But two were still alive. They hit the man and one other who followed him later.

"It was the same in all the dugouts. We found that an officer was alive in one of them.

Colonel Merritt A. Edson, commanding officer of the Marine Raiders, conducts a meeting of his senior officers.

We sent an interpreter out to get him. The interpreter came to the mouth of the cave and asked if the officer wanted to surrender. The answer was a grenade."

Despite opposition and casualties, the Raiders drove down the ridgeback of the island until they ran into a shovel-shaped ravine with three steep sides. Here they met the stiffest Japanese resistance. The walls of the ravine surrounded a flat space that the British, in peacetime, had used as a cricket field. Now the Japanese had dug innumerable large caves into the limestone walls of the ravine, and from the narrow mouths of these dugouts they fired rifles, automatic rifles, and machine guns. There was "continuous crossfire across the ravine," said the colonel.

By the time the marines reached this area, it was dusk and they halted for the night. But the Japanese were organizing a counterattack.

"At ten thirty that night the Japanese counterattacked," said the colonel. "They broke through between C and A companies, and C Company was temporarily cut off. The Japanese worked their way along the ridge and came to within fifty to seventy-five yards of my command post. They were using hand grenades, rifles, and machine guns. We suffered quite a few casualties as our men fought hard to hold them back. One machine gun company lost fifty percent of its noncommissioned officers. Finally the enemy was thrown back.

"The next day the Raiders, aided by support troops under Colonel Rosecrans [Harold E. Rosecrans of Washington, D.C.], cleaned up the southeastern end of the island.

"The Japanese were still in the pocket [in the cricket-field area]. But we had positions for machine guns and mortars on three sides of them. We closed in on the pocket and cleaned up some of the dugouts. By three o'clock that [Sunday] afternoon we had complete physical control of the island. A few groups of snipers and machine gunners remained. It took days to finish them off.

"The Japanese defense was apparently built around small groups in dugouts with no hope of escape. They would stay in there as long as there was one live Japanese soldier. There was a radio for communication in nearly every one of these holes.

"We pulled out thirty-five dead Japanese from one dugout. In another we took out thirty. Some of these people had been dead for three days. But others were still in there shooting.

"In none of these places was there any water or food. They had evidently made a dash for their dugouts when the naval bombardment came, without stopping for provisions.

72

"In one case there were three Japanese cornered. They had one pistol. They fired the pistol until they had three shots left. Then one man shot the two others and killed himself."

Colonel Edson listed some of the outstanding heroes among his Raider troops. Major Kenneth D. Bailey of Danville, Illinois, had acted with great bravery in trying to knock out a Japanese dugout emplacement that was holding up our advance.

"The cave was dug in the ravine," said the colonel. "The enemy fire was so severe that our men could not advance.

"Bailey got on top of the cave by crawling. He tried to kick a hole in the top. When that failed, he tried to kick the rocks away at the foot of the entrance. While he was attempting to do that, one of the Japanese stuck out a rifle and shot him in the leg."

Then there was Gunnery Sergeant Angus Goss, a one-man demolition squad. When the Japanese in one cave had resisted with particular stubbornness, Sergeant Goss had tried throwing in hand grenades. These had been promptly returned by the Japanese inside. The sergeant then tried holding the grenades for three seconds before hurling them, but the Japanese caught the missiles and threw them back. The patient sergeant then got TNT and thrust it into the hole. The trapped men shoved the TNT out of the cave and the dynamite exploded outside, driving splinters into Goss's leg. He then "got mad," went into the cave firing full tilt with his submachine gun, and killed the four Japanese who were still alive. Eight other dead Japanese were found in the dugout.

Bob Miller and I were anxious to visit the Gavutu and Tanambogo battlegrounds and secured permission to go. There a battalion of marine paratroops, landing from boats, had hit fanatic opposition and conquered it. We went in a type of boat called a Higgins. Our guide was a sturdy young man in jump boots, Captain George R. Stallings of Augusta, Georgia.

Captain Stallings told us the stories of some of the heroes of Gavutu as we climbed the exceedingly steep hill on the island. One of the first marine casualties, he said, had been Major Robert H. Williams of New Bern, North Carolina, who had led the first wave of troops trying to storm this very hill.

But the outstanding hero had been Captain Harold L. Torgerson of Valley Stream, Long Island, who had blasted many Japanese caves with homemade dynamite bombs. His method was to tie thirty sticks of dynamite together, run to the cave mouth while four of his men covered it with rifles and submachine guns, light the fuse, shove the TNT in among the

Japanese, and then run as fast as he could.

In his day's work Captain Torgerson had used twenty cases of dynamite and all the available matches. His wristwatch strap had been broken by a bullet that creased his wrist. Another grazing bullet had struck his rear end. But that did not stop his fiery campaign.

On one occasion, said Captain Stallings, the wild and woolly Torgerson had attached a five-gallon can of gasoline to one of his homemade bombs "to make it better." That bomb went off with a great roar, knocked Torgerson down,

A soldier struggles through heavy vegetation on his way to the front lines.

and blasted away most of his pants—as well as blowing in the roof of a Japanese dugout.

We rode in a boat from Gavutu to Tanambogo, bypassing the long connecting causeway, where the marines had tried without success to effect a crossing. We landed on the Tanambogo docks, where other marine troops had finally come ashore. We passed two burned-out tanks. These, said Captain Stallings, were the vanguard of the American landing. The defending Japanese had jammed the treads with crowbars, swarmed over the tanks, and set them afire with rags soaked in gasoline.

"The Japanese screamed and hollered and actually beat on the tanks with their fists and knives," said Captain Stallings. One of the tank commanders, he said, had opened the hatch and killed twenty-three of the enemy with a machine gun before he was stabbed to death. "I counted the bodies myself," said Stallings.

On a board ramp on the Tanambogo shore, we saw the remnants of two of the Zero float planes that had been set afire by our strafing navy fighters.

Then it was time to go back to Tulagi. The sun was beginning to go down and the coxswain of our boat was growing more and more anxious.

Back at Tulagi there is business to attend to.

76

We are scheduled to leave for Guadalcanal at 4:30 tomorrow morning, and I want to make sure that we will have a fast boat for the return trip. I am certain that the enemy submarine that chased us today will be lying off the harbor entrance, waiting.

THURSDAY, AUGUST 13, 1942

We were up at four this morning and down to the dock in the dark. The night had turned cold, as is usual in this climate. The sky had been blacked out by a low overcast.

There were two boats in our fleet. One was our own landing boat; the other, a lighter that was carrying Japanese prisoners back to Guadalcanal. The prisoners, their hands up, were led into the small hold of the lighter.

There were ten prisoners, three of them navy troops, the other seven uniformed laborers. They took their places silently, obediently, as if they expected to be taken out into the bay and drowned, and were resigned to their fate. Two of them later told an interpreter that they had expected to be killed when captured.

And so we started out, showing a pre-arranged signal to warn outposts against shooting at us. And once past the line of sentries we crept along at a low speed, hugging the cover of the shoreline. The water was rough, and despite our low speed, we were drenched by spray.

At about five o'clock we thought the jig was up. A white point of light like a bright star appeared in the sky to the south, and then the star burgeoned into a greater brightness, casting a flickering sheet of light over the whole sky. It was a flare. The sub, we thought, was looking for us.

Another flare, closer and more directly ahead of us, followed a few moments later. We went through several maneuvers, like running along the edges of rocks and shutting off engines, to confuse the enemy. At the moment they were probably listening to our propeller beat and trying to fix our location through their detector.

We resumed our course some fifteen minutes later, and there were no flares. But several times more we went through maneuvers designed to throw off the enemy.

It was six o'clock in the morning, and the sky was growing uncomfortably light, when we passed the last protecting shoulder of land and headed out into the open bay. There would be no land within easy swimming distance now until we had nearly finished our trip. This was our dash for life; the coxswain opened the throttle wide and we pounded hard into the short, high, choppy waves. Solid water began to sluice over the bow in sheets. We were drenched anew with each wave, and the wind was chilling, but we did not slow down. This was no time for comfort.

Somewhere we had lost a lot of time and fallen far behind our schedule. We had planned to be out in the middle of the bay by 6:30. But at that time we were only a few hundred yards away from the shores of the Tulagi group of islands.

Yet the submarine—we thank our stars—did not appear. We found out later that he had been sighted across the bay, along the Guadalcanal shore, at about that time.

Halfway across the bay the coxswain turned to me and said, "Our chances are about one in three of getting there now." But whatever our chances at that moment, they had certainly improved greatly. The high, cloud-girdled mountains of Guadalcanal were becoming more and more distinct ahead of us. We would be there soon—if we did not spot a sub.

Then we were close enough to Guadalcanal to see isolated palm trees clearly against the skyline and rows of bamboo shacks. We knew we were going to make it.

·6·
EXPEDITION
TO MATANIKAU

FRIDAY, AUGUST 14, 1942

Enemy aircraft dropped their first bombs on Guadalcanal today. They had been over before, but this was the first time they actually attacked the island.

The time was 12:15, and I was at General Vandegrift's headquarters on one edge of the airfield. I was attempting to catch up with my writing, when an outpost phoned to say the enemy had been spotted. There were eighteen bombers, coming in high.

The air-raid alarm, a dilapidated dinner bell, jangled; and there was a general scurrying for protective foxholes. And we knew the airfield would be the target. And we have no planes of our own to send against the Japanese. Since the Battle of Savo Island, where the four cruisers were sunk, we have no protective fleet either. There is only one battery of small, 90-millimeter anti-aircraft guns.

In a few seconds someone shouted "There they are!" and pointed, and we all looked. Then I saw the first three of the Japanese planes, silvery and beautiful in the high sky. They were so high that they looked like a slender white cloud moving slowly across the blue. But through my field glasses I could see the silvery-white bodies quite distinctly: the thin wings, the two slim engine housings, the shimmering arcs of the propeller. I was surprised that enemy aircraft, flying overhead with the obvious intention of dropping high explosives upon us, could be so beautiful.

We heard a closely spaced series of explosions, sharp and apparently quite near. The sounds were notably loud, and sharper than any I had heard before. And the ground shook under our feet.

The Japanese had dropped six bombs, which had fortunately fallen into the water, near Kukum. The planes swung in a slow circle with anti-aircraft bursting behind them and then disappeared into the sky to the south.

MONDAY, AUGUST 17, 1942

I reached Colonel Hunt's CP (command post) in the late afternoon, to find the colonel at the center of a rather grim group of officers. They were laying plans for a large excursion into Matanikau, and it was easy to see that they are intent on mopping up the enemy in the village this time. The attack will come off the day after tomorrow. The plan is to box in the town from three sides. One company of troops, under Captain Spurlock (Lyman D. Spurlock of Lincoln, Nebraska), will set out tomorrow morning, cut through the jungles to the rear of Matanikau, and work into position for an assault from the land side. Another company, led by Captain Hawkins, will advance along the shore toward Matanikau from Kukum, bivouac overnight, and be in position to strike from the east when the attack begins. A third group of troops, under Captain Bert W. Hardy of Toledo, Ohio, will make a landing from boats far to the west of Matanikau, beyond the next westernmost village of Kokumbona, and attack Matanikau from the west along the shore.

Captain Hawkins's troops will leave Kukum at one o'clock tomorrow afternoon. I asked him if I might accompany his outfit. "Sure," he said. "Come right along."

TUESDAY, AUGUST 18, 1942

Jim Hurlbut (Sergeant James Hurlbut of Washington, D.C.), Bob Miller (the Marine Corps correspondent), and I set out in a jeep for Kukum, to join Captain Hawkins's expedition to Matanikau. This will be the first effort to expand our little beachhead on Guadalcanal. We hold only a strip about six miles long, and three miles deep, around the airfield. The rest of the island, eighty by thirty miles, is assumed to be in enemy hands.

WEDNESDAY, AUGUST 19, 1942

We were awakened several times after midnight by cannonading, but we did not get up.

We reached the clearing with the white trees shortly after eight o'clock and halted there to wait for our own artillery bombardment of Matanikau.

At 8:30 a marine came in from the beach, out of breath, and said, "There's a Japanese destroyer out there." I went to the shore expecting this to turn out to be nothing but a false alarm and was startled. Like a toy ship on the horizon, but very distinct, moving in from the sea, was a Japanese warship. With my field glasses I could make out turrets fore and aft, the decks crowded with piles of superstructure, the curved bow, and even an orange flag with a red rising sun at the masthead. One felt naked and helpless when an enemy destroyer could parade so brazenly off our beach, in daylight. If we only had some aircraft we could make him run!

I watched the ship as it slowly swung bow on until it pointed straight for the spot where I stood, kept turning, and swung broadside to shore. It did not fire, and apparently it lay beyond the range of our shore batteries, for they were not firing either.

A few minutes later, as I returned to our troop column, our artillery opened the expected barrage against Matanikau. We heard the booming of the guns behind us, then the soft sighing as the shells passed overhead, and sharp, loud crashes in quick succession as they landed.

We halted and then moved on while the intensity of the barrage increased until the booms of the cannon, the sighs of the passing shells, and the cracks of the explosions overlapped and mingled in a continuous train of sound.

When we halted again, I worked my way to the seaside to find that only the masts of the Japanese destroyer were visible, projecting just above the rim of the horizon toward Tulagi. The ship was firing, I knew; a thin, dirty cloud of smoke floated over the masts. It was the unmistakable smoke that comes with gunfire.

I rejoined our main group of troops just in time to hear a burst of gunfire from our left flank and ahead. There were several bursts of submachine gun fire, then a few rifle shots, and then the sharp answering crack of a Japanese .25 caliber. I knew that sound by this time, and hit the deck in a clump of brush behind a tree. More .25's cracked in rapid succession, and firing went on at intervals. I watched the ants hustling through the foliage under my nose. There were three kinds of ants, large and small red ones and medium-sized black ones. There was little to do except watch them until the firing let up.

It was about 9:45 when the firing lulled, and we poked our heads out into the open again to see what went on. Apparently a sniper or two had been knocked out ahead of us. But we moved cautiously. I was moving forward, along the fairly open edge of the trail, when I heard a .25-caliber machine gun. Then more enemy .25's opened up ahead; a storm of firing broke and filled the jungle.

I dived for the nearest tree, which unfortunately stood somewhat alone and *was not* surrounded by deep foliage. While the firing continued and I could hear the occasional impact of a bullet hitting a nearby tree or snap-

ADMIRALTY
ISLANDS

BISMARCK
ARCHIPELAGO

NEW
IRELAND

NEW
BRITAIN

NEW
GUINEA

N
W E
S

The **SOLOMON ISLANDS** and **NEW GUINEA**

SCALE OF MILES

0   50   100   200   300

PACIFIC OCEAN

BOUGAINVILLE

SOLOMON ISLANDS

SAVO

TULAGI

FLORIDA

HENDERSON FIELD

GUADALCANAL

Coral Sea

ping off a twig, I debated whether it would be wiser to stay in my exposed spot or to run for a better hole and risk being hit by a sniper.

I was still debating the question when I heard a bullet snap very close to my left shoulder, heard it thud into the ground, and at the same time heard the crack of the rifle that had fired it. Two marines on the ground ten or fifteen feet ahead of me turned and looked to see if I had been hit. That made up my mind. I jumped up and dashed for a big bush. It was well populated with ants that crawled up my trouser legs, but such annoyances were secondary now.

The sniper who had fired at me was still on my track. He had spotted my field glasses and had taken me for a regular officer.

I searched the nearby trees but could see nothing moving—no smoke, no signs of any sniper. Then a .25 cracked again and I heard the bullet pass—fortunately not so close as before. I jumped for better cover, behind two close trees that were surrounded by ferns, small pineapple plants, and saplings. Here I began to wish I had a rifle instead of a short-range .45 pistol. I should like to find that sniper, I thought. I had made an ignominious retreat. My dignity had been offended. The Matanikau sortie had become a personal matter.

Marines on their way to the Matanikau engagement.

Then it began to rain hard. It rained until we were soaked and the ground was mushy, while the firing continued.

The word came back from our advance column, via runner, that our troops were pushing ahead to the village. The firing had by this time slackened considerably. There were only a few stray rifle shots to be heard.

But there were still plenty of the enemy about. Suddenly, to our left, we heard a terrific burst of automatic rifle fire, mixed with the reports of rifles and submachine guns. Then silence. And a few minutes later a marine walked down to the trail with a Japanese soldier in tow.

The captured man's face was marked by signs of terror obvious to anybody. The marine guard explained the reason. "There were four of them," he said. "His three pals were cut in pieces."

89

Sergeant Hurlbut, Miller, and I had agreed by this time to return to headquarters. So it was decided that we should accompany the prisoner to the rear, with Sergeant Hurlbut acting as guard.

It was 11:30 when we started, keeping to the edge of the trail. The jungle around us was silent, and we four, three Americans and the Japanese prisoner, were alone. We wondered if we would run into a net of snipers lying in wait for stragglers.

There was one sniper waiting for us. As we came to a bend in the trail, he fired from behind us. We heard the crack of the rifle and the whiz of the bullet, but it did not sound very close. However, we broke into a run, while Hurlbut goaded the prisoner along with his

A jeep gone amphibious on a front-line trail near the Matanikau River.

.45. The Japanese was very obliging. He ran faster than we did. He might have been thinking how happy one of his own people would be to kill him, now that he had disgraced himself by being captured.

We got around the bend in the trail before the sniper could fire again. And we met no more of his disagreeable kind.

Back at Colonel Hunt's CP, later in the afternoon, I heard the news that Matanikau and Kokumbona had been taken. (But it was not true. The forces had been pulled back far short of their objective. The Japanese were far stronger than we expected.)

THURSDAY, AUGUST 20, 1942
This afternoon the marines on this island enjoyed a long-awaited treat: the pleasure of seeing our air support arrive. We watched the flights of fighter planes and dive-bombers swing over the airport, then come in for a landing. The powerful roar of their motors was reassuring. It seemed almost unbelievable that we did not have to dive for shelter at the sound.

"That's the most beautiful sight I've ever seen," said one marine.

And I heard an officer say, "Morale's gone up twenty points this afternoon."

•7•
TENARU FRONT

FRIDAY, AUGUST 21, 1942

At about six o'clock the sky was beginning to lighten in the east, when we heard the sound of airplane engines.

"Ah," said Lieutenant Wilson, "airplanes!" And he rubbed his hands as before a feast. Our planes were warming up.

We had been trying to get through a call to General Vandegrift's headquarters to find out what was happening. Now Lieutenant Wilson tried again and got an answer.

"The firing was all prearranged barrage," he reported. "The enemy front line is the Tenaru."

It was a slight shock to hear the news. If the enemy front lay on the Tenaru River, then a formidable invasion force was probably only three or four miles from the airport, to the east, trying to break through our defenses.

Immediately after breakfast I went down to General Vandegrift's headquarters to seek out Colonel Jerry Thomas. He is operations chief and the sparkplug of our troops in the Solomons. I wanted to check the matter of the Japanese invasion with him. I still found it hard to believe that a large-scale assault had begun.

Colonel Thomas confirmed the story. The enemy had apparently landed in force and made their way down the coast from east to west until they reached the Tenaru River. There they had run into one of our outposts. A fierce exchange of firing had followed, and the Japanese had charged across a narrow spit of sand that closed the mouth of the Tenaru. Fortunately they had run into barbed-wire entanglements. These, and our own fierce resistance, had slowed them down until more troops could be brought into the gap.

"I'm going down to Colonel Cates's CP now," Colonel Thomas said. "Do you want to come?"

Colonel Clifton B. Cates was the commanding officer of the First Marine Regiment, which held our front line along the Tenaru. I said that I would certainly like to go.

We jumped into a jeep and hurried along the road to a tent camp. Colonel Cates was a quick-moving, quick-speaking, very trim and neat man of middle years. I knew that he had won honors in World War I. He and Colonel Thomas went into a quick huddle on the battle then going on. Colonel Cates unfolded a map and pointed to it with a pencil. The scene was very calm, considering that a battle for Guadalcanal was going on only a short distance away.

A grizzled man with a lined face and light blue eyes came up. He was wearing breeches and high laced boots, and his shirt was wet with sweat. Evidently he had been out in the bush. He was Colonel L. B. Cresswell of College City, Louisiana.

Colonel Thomas nodded. "You know this terrain, L.B.," he said without further ado, pointing to the map. "How are the chances of getting tanks in there?"

Colonel Thomas marked out the Japanese position on the map. The enemy forces were evidently concentrated in a fairly small area running along a strip of Guadalcanal's northern shore. Their front was the Tenaru River, which runs roughly north and south in Guadalcanal. The shoreline runs east and west.

Colonel Cresswell would take his troops— and tanks if he could get them through—and move around the southern flank of the enemy position. Then he would drive northward, pushing the enemy toward the sea.

Meanwhile, the American marines who held the line of the Tenaru River under the command of Lieutenant Colonel Alvin Pollock would prevent any further enemy advance. Thus, the enemy would be boxed in from two sides.

"I want you to get in there and pin these people down," Colonel Thomas told Colonel Cresswell. "It's between you and Al [Colonel Pollock]."

Colonel Thomas had climbed into his jeep again and was starting back to the general's headquarters. Did I want to go back? he asked. While I was trying to make up my mind, I was half listening to Colonel Cates, who had just taken a telephone call. "Good work," he was saying. "A white flag, eh?" He turned to me. "The Japanese are coming across with a white flag," he said.

"I'll stay here awhile and maybe go up to the front," I told Colonel Thomas.

"Okay," he said. "Good luck."

His jeep ground into high speed.

"Hold your fire and tell the men to take them prisoner," Colonel Cates was saying into the phone. Then he hung up.

"It's just one man coming over with a white flag," he said. He called Captain Wolf, the in-

95

terpreter attached to his troops. He instructed the captain to go up to the Tenaru front and talk to the prisoner, who was wounded. I started out for the front with Wolf.

We walked several hundred yards through a former coconut grove until we came to an advance command post. The firing sounded quite loud here and I noticed that the men of the command post were stretched out flat on the ground.

"Better get down," advised one of them.

Wolf and I took the hint and squatted in the dirt.

One of the officers was talking on the phone. "All right," he said. "We'll send a couple of men out to check it." He turned to the troops and said, "Our line to Colonel Pollock is out. Mortar fire probably clipped it. Who'll go?"

Two marines, looking scared but resolute, offered their services. They turned to Wolf and me. "We'll show you the way to where Colonel Pollock is, if you'll follow us," they offered.

So we started out, moving fast, keeping low, halting behind trees to look ahead. The marines found the break in the line and set to work to repair it.

"Colonel Pollock is up that way," they said, pointing toward the Tenaru. "He's right out on the point."

Now Wolf and I moved with even more

caution than before, running bent from the waist as we made our way from tree to tree. Snipers were firing occasionally. We heard the crack of their guns, and bullets ricocheting among the trees. Our artillery was ranging on the Japanese positions on the far side of the Tenaru. And the enemy were throwing rifle grenades over to our side. We could see one of the bursts ahead, a spray of dirt rising where the explosive hit. Occasionally we heard the bursts of sharp-sounding Japanese machine gun fire.

We pushed ahead, moving between bursts of firing until we could see the river and the long, curving spit of gray sand that closed its outlet into the sea, and the shadowy coconut grove across the river where the Japanese were.

We were crouching behind a tree when Colonel Pollock, looking quite calm and walking erect, came over. Apparently he wasn't at all afraid of the sniper fire. "The prisoner's up there," he said. He pointed to a group of three or four men lying prone around a foxhole about fifty feet away.

We made a dash for the foxhole and flopped down beside it. In the foxhole, lying on his back, with one of his arms wrapped in a red-stained swath of bandage, was the Japanese prisoner. He looked dazed and unhappy.

Captain Wolf immediately began to talk to

him in Japanese. But the prisoner's answers were slow and apparently not very satisfactory. A marine told me the prisoner had got up from a foxhole and walked across the intervening no-man's land all alone. "Like a ghost," he said. "Or somebody walking in his sleep."

The prisoner said he did not think the others would surrender. When asked how the invaders had arrived on Guadalcanal, he was very vague. He either knew nothing or would say nothing about the ships on which they had arrived on Guadal. (One reason for his confusion became apparent later, when it was learned from other prisoners that the troops, new arrivals, were not told where they were or where they were going. Some of them did not even know they were on Guadalcanal.)

It was only about a hundred yards from the foxhole where the prisoner lay to the front line of the Tenaru River.

Snipers began to range on us from across the river. We heard the *ping-ping-ping* of their .25's, and bullets began to whirr fairly close. I lay still for a few moments while the firing continued, thinking what a wonderful target we were, gathered so close together in a small circle. Then two of the other onlookers and I got the same idea at the same moment and we headed for cover.

A pink-cheeked captain shared my coconut tree. He told me, while we watched the shadowy woods across the river, that it was his unit that had been doing the fighting in this particular sector. His name was James F. Sherman, and he came from Somerville, Massachusetts. "Lots of Boston boys in the outfit," he said. "That's Hell Point, where the Japanese tried their crossing. Some of our men moved up onto the point to get a better field of fire, and the Japanese put up flares that were as bright as daylight. We lost some people in there. But," he added, "we stopped them."

One did not have to look hard to see that he was understating the case. I worked my way to Hell Point, crawling between volleys of firing, flopping close to the earth when a mortar shell or grenade burst, and looked out on hundreds of Japanese bodies strewn in piles.

It was easy to see what they had tried to do. They had tried to storm our positions on the west bank of the river by dashing across a sand bar that was about fifteen feet wide and ten feet above water level. Many of them had come close to reaching their objective. But they had run into unexpected rows of barbed wire on our side of the Tenaru.

"That wire maybe saved the day," said a marine lying next to me.

I looked across the river into the shadowy coconut groves, where only 150 yards from us the advance elements of the enemy were located. We could hear the crack of rifle and machine gun fire from there, and the occasional crash of our own artillery shells falling among the enemy positions. But no Japanese were visible—and that, I had learned, was a perfectly normal condition in this jungle warfare. Rule Number One was to stay under cover.

I heard the report of a sniper's rifle coming from the right, very close, on our side of the riverbank. The sound seemed to come from above. I saw a marine run, crouching, from one tree to the foot of another, and stand peering up into the tree with his rifle ready.

Then, silently as a ghost, he beckoned to another marine, who then zigzagged his way to the foot of the same tree. The second marine had a tommy gun. The first marine pointed up into the foliage, and the second followed the gesture. Then the marine with the tommy gun made his way to a nearby stump and crouched behind it, watching the treetop. I resolved to watch him ferret out the sniper and bring him to earth, but my attention was distracted by the sound of a .25-caliber machine gun coming from the sand bar that closed the mouth of the Tenaru.

"There's a bunch of Japanese on the lee side

Garbed in a captured Japanese sniper's outfit, a marine shinnies up a coconut tree to lie in wait for the unsuspecting enemy.

The marines capturing their first Japanese prisoner.

of the bar," said the marine next to me. "They open up every hour on the hour from behind it. We can't spot 'em."

I could see how it might be possible for the Japanese to hug the lee side of the bar without being seen by our people. The bar was curved in a gentle arc toward the sea, and the bar had steep shoulders like an old-fashioned road. The result of this combination of circumstances was that at certain places there was excellent cover.

The machine gun snapped out at us again in a long burst. "If we could spot that guy we could lay mortar fire right on him," said my informant.

The battlefield is full of distractions. Now I was distracted by heavy firing from our own rifles, coming from my left. I saw a line of marines, lying close together behind sandbags, firing out to sea.

Out in the glassy blue river, globs of water shot up where the bullets struck. "There's a Japanese soldier out there," said my friend. "He's trying to swim around and get in behind us. We've killed a lot of 'em that way."

A veritable sheet of bullets was smacking into the water. Apparently every marine was anxious to shoot at the enemy.

I worked my way back to Captain Sherman, who was standing behind a tree with Colonel

Pollock. Pollock still looked calm and efficient as he trained his field glasses on the patterned rows of coconut trees across the river.

There were bright yellow explosions in the grove now, and a haze of white smoke drifted among the trees. From the back of the grove came heavy fusillades of rifle and machine gun fire.

Colonel Pollock looked at his watch. "Cresswell's probably coming in," he said.

Machine guns began to clatter on our right. "They must be trying to cross the river down there," said Captain Sherman. He told me how, in the darkness of the early morning today, some of the Japanese had tried to cross the Tenaru lagoon by swimming.

Some of them, he said, had reached our side and hidden themselves in an abandoned tank that lay on the sloping riverbank. They had set up a machine gun nest in the tank and it had taken some hours' effort to get them out. I could see the gray bulky shape of the tank up-angled on the slope.

"That machine gun in the tank made it tough for the marines to man that field piece," said Captain Sherman. He pointed to an artillery piece on the riverbank. "They could take that thing in cross fire," he said. "Every time one of our men moved into position to fire the gun, he got shot."

I remembered then that during the first heavy outburst of firing in the early morning, I had heard the loud *bang-bang-bang* of the field piece, slower and heavier than the fire of a machine gun, and then had not heard it again for an hour or two.

At about 1:15 Colonel Pollock announced to the troops, "Our people are coming in at the rear now. I can see 'em. Keep your fire down." He walked erect along our front firing line, saying, "Keep your fire down. These are our people coming in the rear." Rifle and machine gun fire still cracked on the other side of the river; grenades and mortar shells were still bursting among us; but Colonel Pollock was as cool as if he were leading a parade-ground maneuver.

The volleys of machine gun and rifle fire from the depths of the grove across the river grew louder. Colonel Cresswell's people were rolling the enemy toward us.

Suddenly I saw the dark figures of men running on the strip of beach that bordered the palm grove. The figures were far off, possibly a half mile down the light ribbon of sand, but I could see from their squatness that they were Japanese. There was no time for any other impression. In a few seconds the black, violently moving blobs were squashed down on sand and we heard a fusillade of rifle fire. The Japanese did not get up again. It was the first visible evidence that Cresswell's men were completing their maneuver of encirclement.

We knew that from this time on things were going to grow hotter along the Tenaru. It was possible that, as the Japanese were pushed in from the rear, they might charge our positions on the west bank of the Tenaru, might again try to take the spit of sand across the Tenaru mouth.

Two ambulances had come up and stopped well back of our front line. The bearers were now picking up casualties on stretchers, loading them on the ambulances. Colonel Pollock said to me, "The ambulances are going back. You can ride if you want to." I decided to stay and see the excitement.

The colonel passed the word along the line that there should be no firing unless a specific target was visible. The men had just such a target a few moments later when a single Japanese soldier jumped out of the underbrush just across the Tenaru and made a dash for the beach. A storm of firing burst from our line, and red streaks of tracers zipped around him. He dropped to the ground, and for a moment the firing ceased. Then he was up again and running wildly for his life, and the firing was louder than ever. This time he fell violently, on

105

the beach, and did not get up again.

Now the .25-caliber Japanese machine gun that had been shooting at us for hours from the lee side of the Tenaru was opening up again. As usual, it had the effect of making us keep cover and to a certain extent pinning us down. But this time we spotted the troublemaker. A sharp-eyed marine saw a hand move above the level of the top of the sand bar, and made a mental note of the exact spot.

Then one of our mortars went into action. We heard the *thwung* sound of the piece discharging, waited long seconds while the projectile arched into the air, then felt the ground shake as the explosive struck the sand bar and blew up.

We could hear a marine shouting, giving the mortar crew directions for correcting their range. Then again came the *thwung* and the shattering explosion.

"That's better!" called a marine. "Up fifteen!"

The mortar went off again, and just after it was discharged, the figure of a man popped up from behind the spit of sand. He was less than 150 feet from me. I saw him take about three fast steps, and then the mortar shell landed almost directly on top of his helmet. The explosion resulted in a canopy of dirty gray smoke and debris that came down on the Japanese soldier from above, and then he was swallowed up altogether.

The puff of the explosion expanded over the ground, and as it spread and thinned, we saw three more Japanese, evidently members of the same machine gun crew, leap up and start to run for the far end of the Tenaru sand spit.

They had gone only a few feet when they were in clear view of our troops. In another instant bullets, including tracers from our machine guns, were winging all around them. Two of them fell as the fusillades of firing rang out. One kept running, then dived for cover.

When the third one jumped up again, our men were waiting for him. Apparently he sensed this, for he ran desperately, turning in a fast hundred yards in his dash for the far end of the spit. Before he reached it, however, the bullets caught him and knocked him down. I was not sorry to see the end of the last of this machine gun crew. War takes on a very personal flavor when other men are shooting at you, and you feel little sympathy at seeing them killed.

Just then a rumbling of powerful motors came from behind us. We turned to see a group of four tanks moving down the trail through the coconut palms and heading for the Tenaru and the spit of sand across its mouth. The plan, evidently, was to send the tanks across the spit and into the Japanese positions at the edge of the grove.

On our bank of the Tenaru, the tanks halted for a few moments, then plunged on across the sand spit, their treads rattling industriously. We watched these awful machines as they plunged across the spit and into the edge of the grove. It was fascinating to see them bustling amongst the trees, pivoting, turning, spitting sheets of yellow flame. It was like a comedy of toys, something unbelievable, to see them knocking over palm trees which fell slowly, flushing the running figures of men from underneath their treads, following and firing at the fugitives. It was unbelievable to see men falling and being killed so close, to see the explosions of Japanese grenades and mortars, black fountains and showers of dirt near the tanks, and to see the flashes of explosions under their very treads.

We had not realized there were so many Japanese in the grove.

Group after group was flushed out and shot down by the tanks' canister shells.

Several times we could see our tanks firing into clumps of underbrush where Japanese machine gun nests were located. And we could hear the rattling of guns in answer to the heavier banking of the tanks' cannon.

While all this was going on, I saw a bright orange flash, amidst a cloud of black smoke, bursting directly under the treads of one of the tanks, and saw the tank stop suddenly. It was crippled. The other tanks moved in protectively toward it. I learned later that they were taking off the crew, who escaped uninjured.

The three remaining tanks continued to roar and rattle in the palm grove for what seemed hours. They turned everywhere in their swiveling course, their cannons spewing sheets of orange flame. It seemed unlikely that any life could exist under their assault.

I remember seeing one Japanese in particular who was flushed out from under the treads of one of our tanks. He jumped up and ran hard toward the beach, with the tank following. I thought the tank would run him down or hit him with machine gun fire, but it turned off quickly and headed back into the heart of the grove.

The Japanese, however, continued to run. He was heading for the beach. All along our front line, rifle fire banged and machine guns clattered; the tracers arched around the running soldier. It's hard to hit a moving target with small-arms fire.

As the Japanese sank into the underbrush and took cover, Colonel Pollock shouted to his troops, "Don't shoot! You might hit our own tanks."

The fleeing Japanese jumped up and ran another forty or fifty feet toward the shore, then sank down into cover again. Despite the colonel's warning, several rifle shots were fired at him. As usual, each marine was eager to kill his man.

"One man fire!" shouted Captain Sherman. He designated a grizzled, leather-faced marine to do the shooting. I noticed that the man wore the chamois elbow pad and fingerless shooting glove of a rifle-range marksman. The marines told me he was Gunnery Sergeant Charles E. Angus of Nashville, Tennessee, a distinguished marksman who had won many a match in the States.

We watched Sergeant Angus as if he were the spotlighted star of a play when the Japanese jumped up again and began to run. Angus was nervous. He fired several shots, working his bolt fast, and missed. He inserted another clip of cartridges, fired one of them. But then the prey had sunk down into cover again.

It was a little disappointing, but only for the moment. The Japanese had flopped on the beach. He was evidently heading for the sanctuary of the water, hoping to swim for it. But now he started to get up again—and that was

110

as far as he got. He had reached only a crouch when Sergeant Angus, now quite calm, took careful aim and let one shot go. The man sank as if the ground had been jerked out from underneath him. It was a neat shot—at about two hundred yards.

Now the tanks, their job finished, were rolling out of the grove, heading for the spit. There were only three of them left. One sat very still and useless in the grove.

In a few minutes the tanks were behind our line. I followed them back until they stopped a few hundred feet west of the Tenaru, and the tank captain, his face grimy and his shirt soaked with sweat, climbed out. He was Lieutenant Leo B. Case of Syracuse, New York.

Colonel Pollock had come back to talk to Lieutenant Case. The colonel said, "Man, you really had me worried." He laughed. "But what a job!"

The colonel told me that his orders to Lieutenant Case had been only that the tanks should run up and down the beach, on the far side of the Tenaru, and do a sort of reconnaissance (survey). It had been the lieutenant's own idea to turn into the grove, where close-spaced trees made it difficult for tanks to maneuver, and blot out the Japanese positions with point-blank fire.

Veterans of the Tenaru River battle stand beside their light tank.

Marines on patrol up the Tenaru River search for hidden Japanese artillery.

I went back to our front line, for firing was growing heavy again. Across the river one Japanese after another jumped up from the underbrush and dashed for the shore. It was their last hope for escape, for Colonel Cresswell's troops were coming in from behind. Most of the enemy were knocked down by our fire as they ran, long before they reached the beach. Some of them, however, reached the beach and tried to swim away. Their heads, small black dots among the waves, were difficult targets to hit. But whenever our men could see the head of a swimming man, they fired and a storm of little waterspouts rose around the man as the bullets smacked home.

Now we could distinctly see a few green-uniformed marines, noticeably bigger than the enemy, popping into view and then disappearing in the grove across the river, far back among the even lanes of trees. And the sound of rifle and machine gun fire accelerating told us that there must still be considerable Japanese resistance in the grove.

There were more of our troops on the beach at the edge of the grove, far down across the Tenaru. They were visible for a few seconds at a time as they moved forward, then took cover, then repeated the process.

Our artillery fire, which had been pounding into the grove constantly in the earlier part of the day, had now halted. But Colonel Cresswell's people were using mortars to finish off the Japanese. The flashes of the explosions were like huge orange flowers. We simply kept our heads low and watched the excitement. There was no firing from our side of the river, for we were afraid of hitting our own men. And the Japanese were too occupied with fighting our people closing in the rear to bother with those of us on the west bank of the Tenaru.

From time to time a live Japanese soldier stirred from among the dead piled on the Tenaru River spit and dived into the water. But at such point-blank range these would-be escapers did not get far. From Hell Point, on Colonel Pollock's end of the spit, volleys of firing sprang out and the enemy soldier was killed as he swam. Even the kindliest marine could not let a swimming Japanese escape, for then he might swim around to our rear and throw grenades, as several others had done earlier in the day.

There was bitter fighting now in the grove across the Tenaru. We realized that the tanks had not mopped up completely, for we could still hear the snapping of Japanese machine gun and rifle fire. But Colonel Cresswell's people were closing in fast. A large group of them advanced steadily but cautiously down the beach bordering the grove. Several groups moved simultaneously among the rows of palms scarcely three hundred yards beyond the Tenaru. We kept our heads low, for the bullets of Cresswell's marines might accidentally strike among us.

And then, suddenly, the fighting seemed to have ended. We saw three marines at the opposite end of the Tenaru spit swiveling their heads about, stepping tensely with rifles at the ready—all set to kill any Japanese who might try one last stealthy act of resistance.

Several times, as these three leaders moved across the spit, live Japanese stirred among the piles of dead. I was told later that some of them tried to throw grenades at our people—and were killed for their trouble.

Enemy "dead" are dangerous, for there are usually some among them alive enough to wait until you pass, then stab or shoot you. Our marines had by this time learned to take no chances. The dead were shot again, with rifles and pistols, to make sure.

More marines trickled out of the coconut grove from the other side of the Tenaru, following the three leaders, and advancing just as cautiously. More of our men moved out from our side of the Tenaru and crossed the spit to help in the brutal but necessary re-butchery of the dead. I watched our men standing in a shooting-gallery line, thumping bullets into the piles of the Japanese dead. The edge of the water grew brown and muddy. Some said the blood of the Japanese was staining the ocean.

I followed our men out onto the Tenaru spit. At the far end I talked to some of Cresswell's men. They told me there were hundreds of enemy dead in the grove and beyond, as well as a few wounded prisoners.

Just then a new outburst of rifle fire rattled in the coconut grove, followed by a few of the unmistakable sharp cracks of an enemy .25. Snipers were still operating in the grove. We spread out a little on the spit. The strip of sand was not yet a safe meeting ground.

But the Battle of Tenaru was to all intents and purposes at an end. The detailed sequence of the fighting was not yet clear. But we knew that a major Japanese attempt to break through our lines and recapture the airfield had been stopped, and we knew too that this must have been one of the most crushing defeats the Japanese had yet suffered. Our own casualties, I found, were only 100—twenty-eight killed and 72 wounded; whereas the enemy had lost an estimated 700 killed. (I found out later that the actual count of the Japanese bodies in the Tenaru battle area was 871. They had thought they could drive us from our beachhead with only 1,000 assault troops!)

Under heavy sniper fire, four marines carry their wounded comrade to safety.

·8·
BOMBARDMENT

TUESDAY, AUGUST 25, 1942

I was skirting the airfield en route to Colonel Hunt's CP this afternoon when the air-raid alert sounded. A few moments later we heard the impressive sound of many powerful engines and saw the usual thin silver line of Japanese bombers spanning the sky.

There were twenty-one of them this time. I counted them; then, as they were almost overhead, I dashed for shelter behind a huge limestone rock. I heard the bombs coming down, and the swishing sound of their descent was louder than I had ever heard it before. I forgot the approved method of taking bomb cover, which is to support yourself a little on your elbows and avoid concussion. Instead, I burrowed as deeply as possibly into the ground.

The crash of the stick of bombs was loud, and I felt the earth jerk with the impact. Clods of dirt came showering down. When the last *carrummp* had sounded, I waited a few seconds, then got up a bit shaken and looked across the grassy field at a row of fresh, clean-cut bomb craters. The ground everywhere around was strewn with small, cube-shaped clods of earth. I measured off the distance to the nearest crater. It was not much more than two hundred feet.

Tonight I heard cheerful reports of an action between our naval forces and the Japanese somewhere near Guadalcanal. Torpedo bombers from one of our carriers had attacked the Japanese carrier *Ryujo* and probably sunk it. At the same time, seventy-one out of eighty-one Japanese planes had been shot down while attacking one of our carriers. But the carrier, the *Enterprise,* had been badly hit and set afire.

WEDNESDAY, AUGUST 26, 1942

Bob Miller, the United Press correspondent, and I were standing at the edge of the airfield today when the now-routine Japanese air raid occurred. We have our timing during these raids down to a schedule by this time. We know about how long we can afford to watch the bombers before taking cover. Today we heard the bombs screeching down as loud and close as they were yesterday. Then we piled into a small foxhole. This time I remembered to support myself slightly on my elbows, to avoid concussion in case a bomb came too close. Some of our people had been so badly shaken by close ones that they suffered shock and prolonged bleeding from the nose.

The worst time in a bombing is the short moment when you can hear the bombs coming. Then you feel helpless, and you think very intensely of the fact that it is purely a matter of chance whether or not you will be hit. The chances vary with your location. In other words, when the Japanese are bombing such and such an area, consisting of so many acres, fragments from their bombs will cover a certain proportion of the total acreage. You wonder, then, if your portion of the acreage will be overlapped by the acreage of the bombs.

If you are caught on the airfield during a bombing raid, you can figure that your chances for escaping injury are much worse than elsewhere, for the airport always seems to be the enemy's target. But even in other parts of the island, where the odds may be greater—say, nine out of ten that you won't be hit—you wonder if you will be the unlucky tenth case.

You also think about those who have been

cruelly wounded or killed by previous bomb-
ings, and in your imagination you suffer the
shock of similar wounds. You also wonder
why, instead of getting into a shelter that has a
sandbagged roof, you stayed around to gawk
and left yourself only time to get to an open
foxhole or nothing at all for protection except
the flatness of the earth. When you have nothing but the earth to protect you, you feel sin-
gularly naked and at the mercy of the bombs.

These thoughts pass very swiftly through
your head during the short time that seems so
long, the time when you hear the bombs
swishing and rattling through the air on their
way down to you. And while these thoughts
are racing through your mind, your ears, without any conscious effort on your part, are
straining to gauge the closeness of the bombs
from their swishing and rattling sound.

After the sticks have hit, you wait a few
more moments, having no desire to get up immediately. You watch the ground close in front
of your eyes very patiently, and wait to see if
there will be another stick or more sticks.
Usually, here on Guadalcanal, there are no
more sticks after the bombers have made one
run. They do not come back a second time because they are too busy trying to fend off our
fighters.

When you finally get up to look around, you

have butterflies in your chest and your breath is noticeably short and your hands feel a bit shaky.

TUESDAY, SEPTEMBER 1, 1942
Bob Miller and I went to Kukum at about noon today to watch for an air raid. There was an urgent alert, but the Japanese did not appear. So we went for a swim in the beautiful clear water along Kukum Beach. The swimming was superb, but would have been more

A radio station on Guadalcanal was completely destroyed during a Japanese bombing raid.

enjoyable if we had not found it necessary to look out for sharks. Just as crocodiles are a menace to one's contentment while swimming in the Lunga River, sharks are the principal hazard of swimming in salt water hereabouts—that and the danger of getting fungus infections in the ear.

This afternoon trucks came to dump a pile of gray canvas sacks at Colonel Hunt's CP. It was mail—the first to reach the troops since we landed on Guadalcanal! Each man seemed as happy at the mere thought of getting mail as if you had given him a hundred-dollar bill. And that evening was an orgy of reading. Most of the men had three or four letters each. They sat about in circles and, besides reading them several times, read pieces of them to one another.

SUNDAY, SEPTEMBER 6, 1942
Lieutenant Richard R. Amerine of Lawrence, Kansas, a marine flier, came wandering in to our lines today, thin as a ghost. He had been out in the jungles, dodging Japanese and existing on red ants and snails for several days. He had parachuted from a fighter plane when his oxygen apparatus went out a week ago, and had landed at Cape Esperance on the northwest corner of the island. Trying to find his way back, he had run into a large group of

Japanese troops. He had found one of them asleep by the side of a trail, had killed him by beating his head with a boulder, and had taken his pistol and shoes. Then he had killed two more Japanese with the butt of his gun and still another one with a bullet before finally reaching our lines. Having once studied entomology, the science of bugs, he was able to subsist on selected ants and snails. He knew which were edible.

There's a tide of cheerful scuttlebutt tonight that relief is on the way for the marines here on Guadal, that a huge convoy of ships is en route carrying enough army troops so that the marines will be able to ship out and perhaps go home.

·9·
BATTLE
OF THE RIDGE

MONDAY, SEPTEMBER 7, 1942

This morning Colonel Edson, the commanding officer of the Raiders, told me that he is planning to make an attack on the Japanese positions in the Taivu Point area tomorrow. If I wanted to go along, he said, I was to be at Kukum at 3:45 this afternoon.

It was pelting rain when I arrived. But the Raiders, who seem to love a fight, were in high spirits. I had been assigned by Colonel Edson to go with Lieutenant Colonel Sam Griffith, the second in command, aboard a tiny diesel-engined ship that was acting as an auxiliary transport for the occasion. As we stepped aboard, one happy marine said, "This is the battleship *Oregon*, I presume?"

The captain of the little craft was a jovial Portuguese who had formerly been a tuna captain on the American West Coast. His name, Joaquin S. Theodore. His ship had been a tuna boat. The captain still spoke in interesting Portuguese phrases, despite his rank as captain of a naval ship.

Colonel Griffith later went over the plans for our expedition. We are to land our troops to the east of a small village called Tasimboko, in the Taivu Point area, and advance from that direction on the town. Tasimboko is supposed to be the bivouac of a large group of Japanese troops—estimated to number from one to three thousand. But they are supposed to be lightly armed.

A bombing and strafing attack on Tasimboko, and shelling from the sea, will be timed to fit in with our attack.

Getting to sleep was a terrible job. The ship's steaming hold, full of the noise of the engines, was crammed with marines; no room to sprawl there. Every nook about the deck seemed to be filled as well.

TUESDAY, SEPTEMBER 8, 1942

Despite the hardships of sleeping aboard Captain Theodore's tiny tub, the Raiders were fresh and ready to go before dawn when the

126

time came for us to climb into our boats and shove off for shore.

Just as we were starting, there came a fortunate happenstance. A small convoy of American cargo ships, escorted by warships, passed very close to our own transports. They had no connection with us and were bound for a different part of Guadalcanal; but the Japanese, seeing our ships and the others together, evidently got the impression that a mass assault was coming. And so, fortunately, many of them ran.

But naturally we had no way of knowing this as we dashed for shore in our landing boats. We were ready for a real struggle, and a bit puzzled when there were no shots from shore.

We were more mystified when, a few minutes after landing, we found a fine, serviceable 37-millimeter field piece, with the latest split-trail rubber-tired carriage, sitting abandoned at the edge of the beach. It was complete with ammunition and surrounded by Japanese packs, life preservers, intrenching tools, and new shoes, strewn in disorder on the ground.

As we moved along we found more packs, more shoes and life preservers, and freshly dug slit trenches and foxholes in the underbrush. We also found another fine 37-millimeter gun which, like the other, was unmanned. This second gun was pointed toward the west, indicating that we had probably surprised the Japanese by attacking from the east.

We moved along the shore through an overgrown coconut grove. And in the brakes of underbrush we found more foxholes, carefully camouflaged with palm leaves, and caches of food and ammunition.

Shortly after eight o'clock we made our first contact with the enemy. I saw our people running in numerous directions at once and knew that something had happened. I ran to the beach and saw a row of Japanese landing boats lying on the sand some distance away. Amid the boats was a small group of men in brown uniforms looking our way.

Now they were answering our fire. I heard the familiar flat crack of the .25 rifle, and the repetition of the sound in long bursts of light machine gun fire. Others of our men joined in the firing, and it swelled in volume.

There was a lull for a few moments, and then rifle and machine gun fire burst out again, the Japanese guns standing out in the chorus like a tenor in a quartet. The bullets were closer this time. I crawled under a wet bush and kept my head down.

The foxholes were growing more numerous as we progressed. They were everywhere, carefully camouflaged with leaves and branches.

128

And caches of supplies were also numerous. There were crates of canned meat, sacks of crackers, field knapsacks with shoes strapped to them, and scores of gray life preservers. The latter were an indication that the Japanese troops who had been here were probably freshly landed from boats.

Suddenly something moved in the bush ahead and to our left. "There are troops going through there," said Colonel "Red Mike" Edson. "Find out who they are."

A few minutes later firing burst out again. I flopped into thick cover, and none too soon. A bullet snapped into the underbrush very close behind me. I picked out the sounds of Japanese .25's, our automatic rifles, and our machine guns. There was a torrent of rapid enemy machine gun firing from the left.

"The boys got on the other side of us," said Red Mike, with one of his wry smiles.

Now came a terrific blast from only a few yards ahead. It was so loud it made my ears ring, and the concussion shook chips of wood onto my head from the trees above. We heard the shell whiz just over our heads and burst a few hundred yards to the rear. We knew then that we must be right up against the muzzle of a Japanese field piece.

The piece fired again and again, and then there was another outburst of machine gun fire, ours heavy-toned in contrast to the enemy's cracking .25's. Then there was silence.

There was quite a cluster of us in this little jungle grove. The marines were squatting or sprawling unhappily in the green, wet underbrush. Then it began to rain, and the rain came in sheets and torrents. The firing started up again. There were Japanese riflemen around us too. (I later found out that there had been an enemy rifleman not more than fifty feet from us. We found his body. Why he did not fire at us I don't know.)

I moved off to the right to try to get a look ahead, and then moved to the rear to see what damage the Japanese shells were doing. I passed a marine who was lying on his back in a foxhole, his face very gray. His upper torso was wrapped in bandages, and I could see there was no arm where his left arm had been, not even a stump. A 75-millimeter shell had done the work.

It began to look as if we might have tackled a bigger Japanese force than we could handle. Colonel Edson was concerned about the enemy who might, he thought, be sneaking around our flank, cutting us off from the beach where we had landed. He called for naval gunfire support.

A group of destroyers that had come down with us swung in close to shore and began to shell Tasimboko. I went out to the beach to watch the yellow flashes and the geysers of smoke and debris rising where the shells hit.

By this time it had stopped raining. When the firing stopped, a great quiet fell on the jungle. And in the quiet, we heard the desperate shouting of a man who was evidently in great trouble. He was shouting something like "Yama, yama!" as if his life depended on it. Then the voice was smothered in a fusillade of machine gun and rifle fire. It was a Japanese. But we never found out what he was shouting about.

We marched into Tasimboko without any further resistance. We found many more cases of Japanese food and sacks of rice, and ammunition for Japanese machine guns, rifles, and artillery pieces totaling more than 500,000 rounds. We burned the ammunition and destroyed the village of Tasimboko, including a radio station the Japanese had established there.

Most of the loot we had captured was destroyed. But we transported the medical supplies back to headquarters, and our men helped themselves to large stocks of British cigarettes bearing a Netherlands East Indies tax stamp. (These enemy troops must have been in other parts of the Japanese arc of conquest.)

We marshaled forces on the beach. This time I went aboard the *Little,* an old four-stack destroyer of World War I vintage.

The sun had set and there was only a faint reddish glow on the clouds over the horizon to light the darkening sky when, in our transport ships, we reached a point offshore from the Tenaru River. We were heading toward home.

SUNDAY, SEPTEMBER 13, 1942

We went to bed in our tents tonight, but were shortly told to move out and up to the ridge-top. This time I had enough foresight to take along a blanket and my satchel full of notes. It seemed that another major attack on our beachhead had started, and I didn't want to lose my diary if our camp should be overrun.

We could hear rifle fire coming from our front lines a few hundred yards to the south. Then we heard machine guns. Flares went up occasionally and shed a glow over the sky.

I spread out my poncho and blanket and tried to sleep. I was awakened by the blasting of our own artillery batteries to the north of us. The shells were whirring just over our position in the ridgetop, skimming over the trees, then hitting and exploding a few hundred yards to the south, apparently in the area where the fighting was going on.

132

MONDAY, SEPTEMBER 14, 1942

Shortly after midnight this morning the din of firing grew so tremendous that there was no longer any hope of sleeping.

We were drawing up a strong skirmish line on the ridgetop. Reinforcements were on their way up. We knew that the Raiders, Colonel Edson's people out on the ridge, had their hands full. We were certain then that a major Japanese effort to break through our lines and seize the airfield had begun.

Snipers were moving in on us. They had filtered along the flanks of the ridge and taken up positions all around our CP. Now they began to fire. It was easy to distinguish the sound of their rifles. There were light machine guns, too, of the same caliber. Ricocheting bullets skidded among the trees. We plastered ourselves flat on the ground.

I went to the communications dugout to see if there might be any room inside. But the shack was filled. I picked a spot amidst some sparse bushes at the foot of a tree. A bullet whirred over my head. I moved to another tree.

A stream of tracer bullets arched through the trees from behind us. We heard Japanese .25's opening up from several new directions. It seemed now that they were all around.

The whispered word went around that the

Telephone linemen ford the Lunga River to provide communications facilities for American troops.

Reports from outposts pour into the Guadalcanal message center.

Japanese were landing parachute troops (later proved false). More reinforcements came through our position on the ridge while the enemy were firing. But we wondered if we could hold our place. If the enemy drove down the ridge in force and broke through Colonel Edson's lines, they would be able to take the Division HQ. Unfortunately General Vandegrift's HQ had just been moved from the airfield to a position behind the front line. If the enemy had already cut in behind our position, as we suspected they had, they would box us in and perhaps capture the general and his staff.

But the general remained calm. He sat on the ground beside the operations tent. "Well," he said cheerfully, "it's only a few more hours till dawn. Then we'll see where we stand."

As the first light of dawn came, the general was sitting on the side of the ridge, talking to some of his aides. A Japanese machine gun opened up, and our officers hightailed for the top of the ridge, with me right behind. We were heading for a tent where we would at least be under some sort of cover. Just as we reached the tent, a bullet clanged against a steel plate only two or three feet from us. It was amusing to see the rear ends of the dignified gentlemen disappearing under the edge of the tent. I made an equally undignified entrance.

* * *

It was not safe to walk about the camp this morning. Snipers had worked their way into camouflaged positions in trees through the area, and there were some machine gunners, with small, light .25-caliber guns. You had to watch your cover everywhere you moved.

There were large groups of Japanese on the left or east side of the ridge, in the jungles. There was a lot of firing in that area. We had a firing line of men extending south from the Division HQ, out along the ridge, facing those groups of the enemy. The marines lay along the edge of a road that ran down the exposed top of the ridge, protected only by kunai grass. The Japanese were firing at them from the cover of the jungle.

Beyond that firing line, the ridge curved and dipped. It rose like the back of a hog into a knoll beyond the dip. It was on this knoll that the Raiders had been doing their fiercest fighting.

I worked my way out along the ridge to the firing line, to get a look at the knoll where the Raiders had been fighting. I lay flat next to a machine gunner while the Japanese fired at us with a .25 light gun. A man to our right, farther out on the ridge, was wounded. We saw him crawling back toward us, a pitiful sight, like a dog with only three serviceable legs. He had been shot in the thigh.

Beyond the bend in the ridge, the machine gunner told me, there were several more wounded. A group of six or seven of our men had been hit by machine gun fire. Two of them were dead.

In the jungle at the foot of the ridge we heard our own guns firing as well as those of the Japanese. Some of our troops were pushing through there, mopping up the enemy.

It was evident that the main Japanese attempt down the top of the ridge had failed. I moved out a little farther along the ridge, nearly to the bend in the road where the wounded lay, and I could see the knoll where the fighting had been going on. It was peopled with marines, but they were not firing right now.

We heard the characteristic whine of fighter planes coming. Then we saw them diving on the knoll and heard their machine guns pop and rattle as they dived.

"They've got a bunch of Japanese on the other side of the hill," said a haggard marine next to me. "That's the best way to get at 'em."

I worked my way back to the CP and got some coffee. I was cleaning my mess cup when I heard a loud blubbering shout, like a turkey gobbler's cry, followed by a burst of shooting. I hit the deck immediately, for the sound was close by. When the excitement of the moment

The commanding officer and staff for the Japanese forces during the Bloody Ridge battle.

had stopped and there was no more shooting, I walked to the spot at the entrance to the CP on top of the ridge. There I found the bodies of two Japanese—and one dead marine.

Gunner Banta told me the story. Three Japanese had made a suicide charge with bayonets. One of them had killed a marine and had been shot. A second had been tackled and shot, and the third had run away. These three had been hiding in a bush at the edge of the ridge road, evidently for some time. I had passed within a few feet of that bush on my way out to the firing line and back. The animal-like cry I had heard had been the Japanese "Banzai" shout.

Colonel Edson and Colonel Griffith, the guiding powers of the Raiders, came in to Divison HQ this morning to make a report on the Battle of the Bloody Ridge to General Vandegrift.

The Raider officers' conversations with the general and Colonel Thomas were held in the general's secret sanctum. But I talked to Colonel Edson as he left the shack. He said that the main body of the enemy who had been trying to drive down the ridge had fallen back.

He went on to say that a force of between 1,000 and 2,000 Japanese had tried to storm the ridge, with lesser forces infiltrating along the base. His estimate of their casualties at that time was between 600 and 700 in the ridge area alone. Our artillery fire, he said, had smacked into the midst of a large group of the enemy and wiped out probably 200 of them. Our own casualties had been heavy, for the fighting was furious.

The colonel gave the impression that the big battle of the ridge had ended. The only fighting in the area now was the mopping up of small, isolated Japanese groups by our patrols.

But snipers were scattered through the trees of the area. I had a brush with one of them during today's first air raid.

I was sitting on the side of the ridge that looks over the valley where our tents are located. A throng of Zeros were dogfighting with our Grummans in the clouds and I was trying to spot the planes.

Suddenly I saw the foliage move in a tree across the valley. I looked again and was astonished to see the figure of a man in the crotch of the tree. He seemed to be moving his arms and upper body. He was wearing a camouflaged uniform, the color and texture of coconut husks, to blend into the background. I was so amazed at seeing him so clearly that I might have sat there and meditated about the matter if my reflexes had not been functioning—which they fortunately were. I flopped flat on the ground just as I heard the sniper's gun go off, and the bullet whirred over my head. I then knew that his movement had been the raising of his gun.

But there was no time to reflect on that fact either. I retreated behind a tent. And then anger caught up with me. I wanted to get a rifle and fire at the sniper, even though correspondents are supposed to be noncombatants. Several of our men, however, fired into the crotch of the tree where the sniper was located.

Bob Miller came in from Kukum, where he spent last night. He and I went out on the ridge later in the day to have a look at the Bloody Ridge battleground. We climbed the steep knoll where our troops had made their stand and turned back the main Japanese drive.

The hill was quiet now. Small fires smoldered in the grass. There were black, burned patches where grenades had burst. Everywhere on the hill were strewn hand-grenade cartons, empty rifle shells, ammunition boxes with ragged, hasty rips in their metal tops.

The marines along the slope of the hill sat and watched us quietly as we passed. They looked dirty and worn. Along the flank of the hill, where a path led, we passed strewn bodies of marines and Japanese, sometimes tangled as if they had fallen in a death struggle. At the top of the knoll the dead marines lay close together. Here they had been most exposed to enemy rifle and machine gun fire, and to grenades.

FRIDAY, SEPTEMBER 18, 1942
The rumor that reinforcements were en route

141

to Guadalcanal was substantiated today, when they arrived. Early this morning a certain colonel told me, "I can't say anything more about it, but I'd recommend that you go for a walk on the beach." I went to the beach and saw cargo and warships and transports steaming into sight.

Miller and I went to the landing point to watch the ships unload. All along the beach our weary veterans stood and watched the process passively. We had been talking about reinforcements, and waiting, for a long time.

The reinforcements were marines of the Seventh Regiment. There was boatload after boatload of them. They wore clean green uniforms and new helmets and talked tough and loud as they came ashore.

One of our veterans told me that he had been talking to some of the new arrivals. "These guys want to tell *us* about the war!" he exclaimed. And we knew then it would take some time with these men, as it had with us, to get rid of that loud surface toughness and develop the cool, quiet fortitude that comes with battle experience. But at least the new arrivals were fresh and strong.

Still, we have less than a full division of men on Guadalcanal. No troops can be taken out of this place, except by going feet first. We need all the fighting men we can muster.

Reinforcements arrive to join marines fighting on Guadalcanal.

SATURDAY, SEPTEMBER 19, 1942

I checked over my records in an attempt to find out just how many ships our dive-bombers are credited with having sunk since the first group of planes arrived here nearly a month ago. The total of Japanese ships sunk, I found, is three destroyers, one cruiser, and two transports. Probably a dozen other ships, mostly cruisers and destroyers, have been damaged by hits or near misses. Altogether it is a good score, considering that poor weather conditions and night operations generally make it difficult to spot the location of the enemy.

Still, the enemy landings at Guadalcanal go on. Bit by bit they are building up their forces—despite the recent failure of their second big attack to break through our lines and take the airport. Last night a group of ships came in and shelled us. They probably also landed their daily load of troops.

This afternoon we talked with some of the Raiders about the Battle of Bloody Ridge and heard some interesting stories about the enemy. For instance, several of the Japanese prisoners captured on the ridge said "Knife" when they were captured, and made hara-kiri motions in the region of the belly. But when no knife was forthcoming, they seemed relieved, and after that made no attempt to kill themselves.

WEDNESDAY, SEPTEMBER 23, 1942
"Signs of civilization are coming to Guadalcanal," said General Vandegrift this morning. He told me how an engineer had come into his quarters and asked where he wanted the light. The general said he was surprised to find that

the marine was actually towing an electrical wire behind him. The Japanese powerhouse that we had captured was in working order, and the engineers had extended a line to the general's camp.

The general said that he felt our situation on Guadalcanal was brightening a bit. The Seventh Regiment reinforcements had been a great help, and he seemed assured that the naval protection of our shores would improve. I found out later in the day that a group of motor torpedo boats are on their way to help protect our coastline from the continued Japanese landings.

There is much scuttlebutt about more reinforcements coming into Guadalcanal. But the general feeling seems to be that if army troops are brought in, they will only reinforce, not supplant, the marines, at least for the time being. The old dream of being home for Christmas is fading.

Many of our officers, however, are now being sent home to rest and to train new groups of troops. That is another sign that we have reached a "breather" at least. And the Japanese have confirmed the impression by abstaining from air-raiding us for another day. This evening they failed even to send in the usual landing force of troop-carrying warships, which we call the Tokyo Express.

THURSDAY, SEPTEMBER 24, 1942

We went to the Raiders' CP for breakfast this morning and had a good time yarning over pancakes. We talked about some of the close escapes we have had during this campaign, and Major Ken Bailey, one of the heroes of Tulagi and the battle on the ridge, said something touching about taking chances.

"You get to know these kids so well when you're working with 'em," he said, "and they're such swell kids, that when it comes to a job that's pretty rugged, you'd rather go yourself than send them."

(Major Bailey was killed three days later during a patrol action.)

A rugged marine on Guadalcanal.

·10·
BOMBER TO
BOUGAINVILLE

FRIDAY, SEPTEMBER 25, 1942
I asked the general for permission to leave the
island, and he told me with a chuckle that I
had picked a good time. "They're putting in a
shower for me in a few days," he said. "And
when such luxuries come, the correspondent
should go."

A B-17 came in today, and I asked the pilot,
a very calm, very steady man named Captain
Paul Payne of Des Moines, Iowa, if he would
give me transportation from Guadalcanal to a
certain point to the south, from where I could
make my way back to Honolulu.

Payne said, "Certainly, if you don't mind
going by way of Bougainville." He had orders
to fly a reconnaissance over that forbidding

148

Japanese-held island—a big naval and air base.

SATURDAY, SEPTEMBER 26, 1942

It was dawn when we climbed into the plane. The captain offered me a chocolate bar. "Our usual breakfast," he said. Then the props were wound, the electric starters squealed, and our motors were warming up.

We passed up "the slot" (the much traversed north and south ocean highway between the island rows of the Solomons), looking down at the myriad rugged, jungly islands that slipped under our wings. Time dragged.

We worked our way up amidst the towering banks of cumulus clouds. And finally Captain Payne's voice cracked into my earphones: "Navigator, bearing on Bougainville."

The navigator replied with the bearing. The plane swung in a gentle turn. And ahead of us we saw a black, irregular island mass lying under the clouds.

Then the tail gunner shouted on the communication system: "There's two Zeros coming up behind us!"

From then on we had action.

"They're coming in," said the tail gunner. And after a few seconds, "They've turned off." Zeros are chary of the formidable B-17, but in such a moment as this, one thinks swiftly of our aloneness over enemy territory and the swarms of enemy planes that must be around.

Ahead of us we saw a ship moving, as small as a toy in the distance.

We were moving over the enemy vessel now, and she was putting on knots. We could see the streamers of white foam at her flanks as she plowed at top speed. She was swinging in a circle, trying to dodge the bombs she thought we would rain on her. I imagined the confused scurrying on her decks, having myself been on the decks of ships during bombing attacks. But we were only conducting a reconnaissance, not a bombing.

A gunner reported: "Two planes coming up from below, fast. They're two thousand yards away." And then: "They're turning off."

I saw a plane over on our left. It was a seaplane with a single wing—a Zero float. He was flying the same course we were flying. One of our nose gunners began to fire. The tracer bullets arched around the enemy plane and came closer. The empty shells rattled on the floor of our bomber.

Now the Zero's wing dipped, and he swung in a sharp turn toward us. "Here he comes!" I thought, and I saw the plane sweeping in on us, saw its tracers leaping out. In that instant I thought what I always think in such moments: that I was a fool to get myself into such a spot as this.

Our plane shook as our turret and waist guns took up the firing. The Japanese plane slid by and disappeared to the rear. (We hit him. The rear gunner said the Zero had gone down with its engine knocked out and made a forced landing on the water.)

Other ships were appearing one by one on the water below us. Lieutenant Benjamin was trying to count them, for our main job here was reconnaissance. I saw the long, bristling shape of a cruiser to the right. And there were other ships.

"Anti-aircraft fire to the right!" somebody

A B-17 bomber is shown camouflaged under a skillfully erected net.

shouted. And we heard the fragments thwack against the bottom of the fuselage.

"It looks as if our right aileron's hit," somebody said, but the plane flew well enough.

Then the ack-ack halted, and another Zero popped into sight ahead of us, to the right. He made a three-quarter frontal attack, sweeping in with his tracers reaching for us. The bombardier fired back at him with the nose gun. Our nose compartment filled with smoke from the cartridges. Then the Zero was gone astern.

"Anybody hit?" asked the captain on the intercom.

Nobody answered. These Zeros were poor gunners. They did not come back again.

By this time we were well past the ships that had appeared below us off the southern tip of Bougainville.

"How many ships were there?" asked Captain Payne.

"There were twenty-seven," said Lieutenant Benjamin.

We conducted the rest of our reconnaissance peacefully and ran into no more enemy aircraft or ships. The overcast weather was on our side.

Hours later we landed at an American base that is removed from the Solomon Islands zone and a goodly step toward more peaceful regions.

·11·
VICTORY

That air base where we landed was Espiritu Santo, better known to soldiers, sailors, and airmen by the military code name "Button."

Guadalcanal had a code name too—"Cactus"—but the servicemen preferred to call it "the Canal." The nickname had an affectionate sound about it. Men cursed and hated Guadalcanal, a pesthole that reeked of death, struggle, and disease, but the Canal was like a good-for-nothing cousin or brother. When you make tremendous sacrifices for someone or something, and give your blood or your last drop of muscular effort or sweat, you feel something like affection for that object or person.

Button was not like that. It was only a rear-area base; it was never fought over. Living there was primitive, but compared to the night-and-day misery called Guadalcanal, it was a pleasant rest camp.

At Button I started working over my black-leather diary and began to shape it into this book. Then I went on to New Caledonia, the next base to the rear and the headquarters of the South Pacific force under Admiral William "Bull" Halsey. There I hired a house from a Frenchwoman for a dollar a day and continued writing until I caught a ride by plane back to Pearl Harbor.

Navy officials at Pearl Harbor decided that my black diary was too secret for me to have in my own possession. They were afraid that a spy (and there *were* spies in Hawaii) might steal it or read it. Perhaps they were right, for the diary had accounts of the battles of the Coral Sea and Midway, and the Doolittle raid on Tokyo, as well as Guadalcanal.

At any rate, the navy people took my diary and put it in an office safe at Pearl Harbor. I had to go there every morning and get it from them, work under their noses in that office, and give the book back to be locked up every night.

While I worked from that diary, writing this book, the fighting dragged on and on at Guadalcanal. I wanted to get back there—but from the way the battle was going, I guessed that

154

fighting would continue for many months and that there was plenty of time.

The marines hung on to their little strip of land around the airfield. That strip was only about nine miles long and three miles deep, a tiny toehold on the big island. General Vandegrift wanted to expand this toehold, to take over more of the island, but he didn't have the strength. The marines hung on, waiting for more troops to reinforce them. And almost every night the Japanese blasted them with naval gunfire and bombs. The Tokyo Express ran Japanese troops in to strengthen their forces. In the daytime the Japanese ships and planes stayed in hiding, fearful of our air power. Under cover of darkness they came out to prowl like hunting alley cats.

In October the Japanese mustered their naval, air, and ground strength for another big-scale try at Guadalcanal. They were determined to drive the marines off their tiny beachhead. But first they had to land thousands of troops to strengthen their forces on the island—and before they could make a mass troop landing, they had to weaken our air strength at Henderson Field.

On the night of October 14, a Japanese naval task force, including the mighty battleships *Kongo* and *Haruna,* swung into "Sleepless Lagoon" off Henderson Field and began

155

firing salvos. At short range the big fourteen-inch shells hit accurately, ripped up the runway, smashed planes, killed and mangled marines, and set gasoline stores and ammunition dumps into roaring flames. For an hour and twenty minutes the shelling went on while the marines prayed or cursed. Then the Japanese ships withdrew, leaving more than half of the ninety planes on the airfield wrecked, the gasoline supply almost all destroyed.

October 15 was a sorry day for the marines on Guadalcanal. In bright sunlight that morning, Japanese transports came in to Tassafaronga Point and unloaded troops while the marines looked on helplessly. But in a jungle hiding place, some drums of gasoline were unearthed, tanks of damaged B-17's were drained, and transport planes loaded with aviation gas began to come in from Button. Then, fighting back hard, marines loaded their fighters and bombers with gas, bombs, and machine gun bullets and went out there and smacked the transports. Three Japanese transports were wrecked on the beach, and the Japanese naval force withdrew. But thousands of their troops as well as supplies, guns, and ammunition had been put ashore.

Admiral Nimitz, bossing the entire Pacific naval operation from Pearl Harbor, was gloomy about the future of Guadalcanal. The situation, he said, was critical. And at a still higher headquarters to the rear, in Washington, D.C., Secretary of the Navy Frank Knox said, "Everybody hopes that we can hold on."

I finished my writing job at Pearl Harbor and headed back toward Guadalcanal. Along the line of bases leading to the Solomons, I found some people who felt sure that Guadalcanal would be lost. It seemed that the United States might not have enough strength, at this stage of the war, to support amphibious landings in North Africa, the buildup of military might in England, and the Guadalcanal operation too.

But these people didn't know, and I didn't know, that President Roosevelt had taken a personal hand in Guadalcanal's future. Alarmed by the long tug of war over Henderson Field, he ordered heavy reinforcements to be directed toward the Solomons.

When I reached the area in November, I traveled aboard a big new battleship that had just been thrown into the fight. She was the U.S.S. *Washington,* under Admiral Willis A. "Ching" Lee. She and another battleship, the U.S.S. *South Dakota,* had just fought a knock-down, drag-out fight with two Japanese battlewagons that had been worrying Guadalcanal. In that naval engagement, November 13 to 15, our sea forces had won a narrow victory over a huge fleet of Japanese fighting ships—and some of the pressure was taken off the marines on Guadalcanal.

When I went ashore again on Guadalcanal in December, army reinforcements were there, helping the marines. And the First Marine Division, shot through with battle casualties, malaria, and dysentery, had been bolstered by parts of the Second Marine Division.

Now there were 50,000 American fighting men on the island. Most of the Marine Second Division was there, the Army's 132nd, 182nd, and 164th regiments had landed, and 20,000 more of the 25th (Army) Division were on the way. There were enough troops so that some of the veterans could be given a well-earned rest. Accordingly, early in December, about half of the famed Marine First Division, and the First and Seventh regiments, moved down to the beach, climbed aboard transports, and set sail for a rear area. They had been on the Canal for four months.

A few weeks later, as more army replacements came in, the Marine First and Seventh regiments were able to leave. And General Alexander M. "Sandy" Patch, of the United States Army, took over from the gallant General Vandegrift.

General Patch, with more power on land, sea, and air than General Vandegrift had enjoyed, made plans to expand the small marine beachhead, to drive the Japanese off the rest of the island.

Soon the enemy was showing signs of softening up. Since their big naval defeat their supply lines had been frazzled. Captured diaries showed that they were short of food and ridden by tropical diseases. Now General Patch mounted his first attack, with army troops of the 132nd Regiment and marines of Colonel John Arthur's Second Regiment, Second Marine Division, as a spearhead.

The particular target was a tough one called Gifu. It was a towering mountain mass overlooking Henderson Field—"looking down our throats," as the military men say. Above the field Gifu rose in steep terraces, like the balconies of a big movie theater—and all over them was a thick rug of jungle. The Japanese knew that this was a key position. We found out later that the Japanese officer in charge, Colonel Oka, told his troops to hang on or die fighting. And the Japanese *did* fight that hard.

The American attack jumped off on December 17 and seesawed back and forth over Gifu for three weeks with desperate charges and countercharges.

Finally, supported by heavy artillery and a torrent of 25th Division reinforcements, the Americans swept to the top of the hill and

Planes on Henderson Field during a lull in battle.

Members of a marine parachute battalion, carrying supplies, make their way onto landing barges.

held. At the same time, a drive along the coast was launched, and the Japanese gave way. It seemed that their resistance was broken at last.

Although we didn't know it, the Japanese high command by this time had ordered the evacuation of Guadalcanal. Under cover of night, they sent special troops down and landed them from destroyers, to cover the exit of their main forces. Nearly 12,000 Japanese troops were pulled out of Guadalcanal. In fairness to them, it must be said that the withdrawal was a successful one.

Meanwhile, the 25th Division, under command of Major General J. Lawton "Lightning Joe" Collins, was pushing the Japanese rear guard relentlessly.

On February 9, 1943, six months after the first landing on Guadalcanal, General Patch's aides summoned the correspondents to the Corps HQ and gave us the text of this radio message to Admiral Halsey: "Total and complete defeat of Japanese forces on Guadalcanal effected 1625 today."

So the Guadalcanal campaign ended: six months of blood, sweat, and misery, of nerve and courage winning over horror and fright. On the land and in the air more than 1,600 of our men had died; thousands more had been wounded. In sea battles at least 2,000 more

Americans had given their lives for this small and, until now, unknown island.

Had it been worth this price? In the military sense, definitely yes. On land, sea, and air we had met the best the Japanese had to offer, and we had beaten them decisively. More than 20,000 Japanese had died in the Solomon action—five times as many as we had lost.

But besides breaking the legend of Japanese invincibility, we had taken the first big step on the bloody island-to-island ladder that led to Tokyo and victory.

Throughout the six-month campaign, the Japanese high command recognized the importance of Guadalcanal. But fortunately they kept underestimating our strength and resourcefulness in the Solomons. As late as Christmas, 1942, they believed they would win. The Japanese emperor, Hirohito, said in his public statement for New Year's Day, 1943: "The darkness is very deep but dawn is about to break in the Eastern sky. Today the finest of the Japanese army, navy, and air units are gathering. Sooner or later they will head toward the Solomon Islands, where a decisive battle is being fought between Japan and America."

The decisive battles, however, had already been fought at that time. President Roosevelt realized this when he said: "It would seem that the turning point in this war has at last been reached." The rows of graves on Guadalcanal, the wreckage of a hundred ships in the black depths of Iron Bottom Bay, and our determined fighting forces moving relentlessly northward toward Tokyo—these were the monuments, living and dead, to the turning point, the victory at Guadalcanal.

INDEX

•

Page numbers in *italic type* refer to material in illustrations and captions.

166

167